HOW TO BE A GOOD LEADER

WHEN YOU'VE NEVER HAD ONE

HOW TO BE A GOOD LEADER
WHEN YOU'VE NEVER HAD ONE

The Blueprint for **Modern Leadership**

MICK HUNT
Foreword by LES BROWN

WILEY

Copyright © 2026 by John Wiley & Sons, Inc. All rights reserved, including rights for text and data mining and training of artificial technologies or similar technologies.

Published by John Wiley & Sons, Inc., Hoboken, New Jersey.
Published simultaneously in Canada.

No part of this publication may be reproduced, stored in a retrieval system, or transmitted in any form or by any means, electronic, mechanical, photocopying, recording, scanning, or otherwise, except as permitted under Section 107 or 108 of the 1976 United States Copyright Act, without either the prior written permission of the Publisher, or authorization through payment of the appropriate per-copy fee to the Copyright Clearance Center, Inc., 222 Rosewood Drive, Danvers, MA 01923, (978) 750-8400, fax (978) 750-4470, or on the web at www.copyright.com. Requests to the Publisher for permission should be addressed to the Permissions Department, John Wiley & Sons, Inc., 111 River Street, Hoboken, NJ 07030, (201) 748-6011, fax (201) 748-6008, or online at http://www.wiley.com/go/permission.

The manufacturer's authorized representative according to the EU General Product Safety Regulation is Wiley-VCH GmbH, Boschstr. 12, 69469 Weinheim, Germany, e-mail: Product_Safety@wiley.com.

Trademarks: Wiley and the Wiley logo are trademarks or registered trademarks of John Wiley & Sons, Inc. and/or its affiliates in the United States and other countries and may not be used without written permission. All other trademarks are the property of their respective owners. John Wiley & Sons, Inc. is not associated with any product or vendor mentioned in this book.

Limit of Liability/Disclaimer of Warranty: While the publisher and author have used their best efforts in preparing this book, they make no representations or warranties with respect to the accuracy or completeness of the contents of this book and specifically disclaim any implied warranties of merchantability or fitness for a particular purpose. No warranty may be created or extended by sales representatives or written sales materials. The advice and strategies contained herein may not be suitable for your situation. You should consult with a professional where appropriate. Further, readers should be aware that websites listed in this work may have changed or disappeared between when this work was written and when it is read. Neither the publisher nor author shall be liable for any loss of profit or any other commercial damages, including but not limited to special, incidental, consequential, or other damages.

For general information on our other products and services or for technical support, please contact our Customer Care Department within the United States at (800) 762-2974, outside the United States at (317) 572-3993 or fax (317) 572-4002.

Wiley also publishes its books in a variety of electronic formats. Some content that appears in print may not be available in electronic formats. For more information about Wiley products, visit our website at www.wiley.com.

Library of Congress Cataloging-in-Publication Data is Available:

ISBN: 9781394357956 (Cloth)
ISBN: 9781394357963 (ePub)
ISBN: 9781394357970 (ePDF)

Cover Design: Wiley
Cover Image: © Yellow duck/Shutterstock
Author Photo: Courtesy of the Author
SKY10123493_080525

Contents

Foreword by Les Brown		ix
	Introduction: The Promise	1
Chapter 1	Great Leaders Aren't *Good* Leaders?	19
Chapter 2	False Aspirations: Why You Don't Want to Be a "Great" Leader	31
	Leadership Versus Influence	32
	Don't Be a Try-hard	33
	Rolling It All Up into Good Leadership	40
Chapter 3	The Six Traits of "Great" Leaders Who Aren't *Good* Leaders	41
	Six Ways to Lead Poorly	42
	Bad Leaders Over-delegate and Call It "Empowerment"	48
	What to Take Away from This	52
Chapter 4	The Seven *Because*s of Good Leaders	53
	From *Why* to *Because*	53
	Problems with Starting with *Why*	54
	The Power of *Because*	55
	A Living Because	58
	Being Who You Are in Real Life	61

Chapter 5	Identifying Your Core Leadership Strengths	65
	How to Integrate Non-leader Skills into a Leadership Role	66
	Eight Ways to Stay Great at What You Do While Leading It	67
	Ten Troubleshooting Tips: When You Have No Experience in What You're Leading	75
Chapter 6	How to Speak (and Write) Like a Leader	81
	Good Leaders Talk Like *This*, Not *That*	81
	Reorganizing the C-suite	85
	Leader Voice	88
	Rehearsal (Yes, You Need This)	88
	A Bias Toward Action	89
Chapter 7	How to Cast a Vision People Will Follow	91
	Vision	92
	The Problem a Vision Solves	93
	Visioneering	95
	Be Positive About Your Vision	97
	Les Brown's Impact	99
Chapter 8	How to See the Best in People When They Give You Their Worst	101
	The Pitfalls of Punishment	102
	A Better Route	103
	Kristi's Big Lesson	106
Chapter 9	The Ten Unbreakable Rules for Trustworthy Leadership	109
	Lesson #1: Don't Lie, Even by Omission	110
	Lesson #2: Never Judge in Public	112
	Lesson #3: Never Steal the Credit	113
	Lesson #4: Never Blame	114
	Lesson #5: Never Resist Feedback	115
	Lesson #6: Never Overlook Small Wins	116
	Lesson #7: Never Isolate Yourself	117

	Lesson #8: Never Avoid Difficult Conversations	118
	Lesson #9: Never Overpromise and Underdeliver	120
	Lesson #10: Never Neglect Continuous Learning	122
Chapter 10	How to Bow Out Gracefully	125
	Mark Passes the Reins	125
	The Point of Leaving	126
	How to Be Grateful	127
	Passing the Torch	128
	Avoiding Resentment	129
	Mitigating Regret	130
Chapter 11	Calm, Cool, Collected: Leading Under Intense Pressure	133
	Being Mindful	136
	A Leader's Moment	137
Chapter 12	Your Leadership DNA	139
	The Four Leadership Archetypes	140
Chapter 13	The Vision and Strategy of Apex Leaders	145
	Learn from the Best: Marco, the Apex Leader	146
Chapter 14	The Energy and Momentum of Ignitor Leaders	151
	Learn from the Best: Laquesha, the Ignitor Leader	152
Chapter 15	The Structure and Precision of Forge Leaders	157
	Learn from the Best: Harris, the Forge Leader	158
Chapter 16	The Trust and Collaboration of Nexus Leaders	163
	Learn from the Best: Franklin, the Nexus Leader	164

Chapter 17	The Single Most Critical Insight for Mastering Leadership	171
	You Are a Steward, Not the Star	172
	Team Before Spotlight	173
	Feedback Is Your Best Friend	173
	Conflict Means Growth	174
	Vision Needs Action	175
	The Strongest Mindset Is Resilience	175
	Serve Before Demanding	176
	Stay True to Your Core	177
	Evolve	177
	Own Everything	178

What's Next?	*181*
Tell Me What You Think	*183*
About the Author	*185*
Index	*187*

Foreword

A question has been asked for years: *Are leaders born, or are they made?* Imagine, if you will, a little boy who found himself crying and felt not only his tears coming down his face but also the tears of his mother because of the abuse she was experiencing. And he had gone through this for years, watching. In his heart, he finally said, *This must stop. I must free my mother from this situation.* And that ignited in him a purpose, a drive, a fierceness to become a man.

I've had the privilege of meeting some of the greatest minds in the world, people who inspire the masses to reach beyond what they thought possible. But every now and then, someone comes along who doesn't just inspire; they ignite a fire so deep down within you that you can't help but be transformed.

Michael "Mick" Hunt is that someone; he is that type of leader. Mick has walked a path marked by challenges that could have stopped him in his tracks, but he kept going. He tapped into a resilience and spirit so profound, they could only have come from a promise he made to himself and to his mother. As a young man, he redefined how he saw himself and his life and committed himself to creating a legacy to rewrite his story and build something that his mother, his family, and his community could be proud of. And now, through his life's work, he's helping leaders around the world do the same.

Mick's message isn't just about climbing to the top. It's about discovering your *why*. Nietzsche said that if you know the *why* for living, you can endure almost any *how*. It's about embracing the struggle, for within that struggle lies the very essence of greatness.

Mick understands that true success doesn't come from what we achieve but from the purpose that drives us; from that unstoppable force within each of us that he calls our *because*. In this book, Mick will walk you through principles that have redefined modern leadership, not with hollow buzzwords but with a conviction rooted in hard-earned wisdom and lived experience. He challenges you to throw away outdated notions of leadership and embrace a path that's purpose driven, heartfelt, and impactful.

So, get ready. Let Mick be your guide as you uncover that fire, that reason, that purpose so deeply embedded in your soul that it propels you forward, no matter the obstacles. This journey won't just change the way you lead. It will change who you are. The world needs more leaders like Mick Hunt, people who not only lead but also move us all toward a more empowered, purpose-driven life.

And now, my friend, it's your turn. Keep going. Your best is yet to come.

—Les Brown

Introduction: The Promise

On the morning of December 24, 1988, the world outside buzzed with the vibrant energy of Christmas Eve. Laughter echoed through the streets; homes twinkled with festive lights; and children, bundled in their winter best, played joyously in anticipation of the night's magic. Everywhere, the air was crisp with the promise of celebration, the excitement of the holiday palpable in the cold winter breeze.

Yet within the modest walls of our small home, the atmosphere was starkly different. I sat quietly on the edge of my bed, my ten-year-old self enveloped in a heavy silence that contrasted sharply with the merriment outside. This silence was only broken by the heart-wrenching sobs of my mother, who sat beside me, her tears painting a story of struggle and despair. The sounds of children playing were distant, as if from another world—one where the shadows that loomed over our family didn't exist.

This was no ordinary Christmas Eve for us. It was a defining moment in my young life, a crossroads that would set the path I was to walk for years to come. My mother, a woman who had weathered countless storms of hardship, bore her suffering not as a shroud to hide in but as a stark, unyielding reminder of the battles she had endured. Each tear she shed carved deep emotional canyons through my young heart and, with each drop, a resolve formed within me, pushing me beyond the carefree innocence that defined childhood.

Her tears that day were like rivers, relentless and transformative, shaping the contours of my spirit. They told stories of lost dreams and enduring pain but also of an unspoken strength that had yet to be called upon. As the weak winter sunlight struggled through our threadbare curtains, casting faint shadows that danced quietly around our sparse room, the somber tone of our Christmas Eve was set.

Les Brown's voice, emanating from the old television in the corner, spoke of potential and possibility—his motivational tones a stark contrast to the palpable despair that filled our space. "Shoot for the moon," he urged, his voice rich and persuasive, as if he could sense the weight of the moment. Just then, my mother turned to me, her eyes brimming with a complex tapestry of pain and hope. In her gaze, I saw not just a mother's love but also a warrior's resolve. Her eyes locked onto mine, conveying a depth of unspoken love and fierce determination that rooted me to the spot.

"You are my hope," she whispered, her voice a tremulous thread of sound in the heavy air. "Because I love you, I won't leave." Her words, more than a vow, were an anchor, a declaration of her unyielding presence despite the tempests we faced. This was her profound response to the silent pleas I had whispered night after night for us to escape the dark shadows that haunted our home. Her decision to stay, to fight rather than flee, was laden with a promise—a promise to forge a new path from the thorns of our shared pain.

As she pulled me into her embrace, the chaos of the world outside faded into a distant murmur. In that embrace, as our shared heartache wove a bond that no hardship could unravel, she whispered again, "You can do it." It was more than encouragement; it was an invocation of my potential, a call to rise above our circumstances and claim the destiny that awaited.

In that moment, as her tears mingled with a quiet strength that only those who have faced despair can know, my *because* was born. Not just any promise but a life's mission, crystallized in the crucible of our family's struggles—a vow to transform our shared sorrow into a future replete with joy, to become a pillar of strength my sister could look up to, to embody the virtues of the man I was destined to become.

This early morning of stark contrasts, when the joy of the world outside was shadowed by the pain within our walls, became the foundation of my journey. It was here, in the depths of despair, that the seeds of my future were sown—seeds that would grow into a relentless pursuit of transformation.

On that pivotal Christmas Eve, as I sat engulfed in the shadows of our humble living room, a profound shift occurred within me. A ten-year-old boy's world was irrevocably altered—not by choice but by necessity. In the depths of familial turmoil, amid the quiet sobs of my mother, I felt a part of my childhood slip away, and, in its place, a premature mantle of manhood settled on my young shoulders. It was a transformation born not out of desire but out of an absolute necessity—a must-have change that no child should ever have to endure but one that was essential for the survival and thriving of my family.

"This was not the life I chose, but it was the life that chose me, and I decided to rise—not just to survive, but to prevail," I would later articulate, reflecting on that moment. This realization marked a turning point when *because* became significantly more potent than *why*. It wasn't about why I had to shoulder such a burden—it was because I had no choice but to forge a path forward, a path that promised a semblance of hope and stability for those I held dear.

In the faint glow of daybreak, as Brown's voice continued to resonate through the room, encouraging millions to reach for their dreams, I found my calling not in the dreams of a child but the resolve of a soul forged through adversity. "Change isn't just something you hope for; it's something you seize with both hands and mold into your destiny." This mantra became my guiding light, driving me to transform despair into determination, vulnerability into strength.

The commitment I made that day as a young boy thrust too soon into manhood was sealed by the fierce embrace of my mother, who, in her infinite wisdom, whispered one final directive as I prepared to face the world: "When you shoot for the moon, don't miss." This charge, heavy with the weight of our past struggles and the promise of our future dreams, was not merely a call to aim high but a command to strike true and without falter.

In the tender aftermath of my mother's tears, as her quiet resolve mingled with unwavering strength, the significance of my role not only as a future man but also as a brother became startlingly clear. For my sister, who is three and a half years younger than me, the stakes were just as high. Like me, she endured the emotional storms that swept through our household; like me, she needed a beacon of what strength and integrity should look like in a man.

At that moment, as I absorbed the weight of my mother's resolve and the depth of my own commitments, I understood that my role extended beyond the typical duties of a big brother. I was to be her protector, her guide, and above all, her example of how a man respects, supports, and perseveres. This was not a role I had asked for or one I had anticipated so early in life, but it was one I accepted without hesitation.

"For my sister, I vowed to be more than a guardian; I pledged to be a living example of the virtues we both deserved to see in the world," I would often reflect, recognizing the dual responsibility I carried for both her and our future. My commitment to her was to demonstrate daily the character of the man I aimed to become, to show her through actions, not just words, what it meant to respect and uplift others, even amid our own struggles.

This nuanced understanding of my role reshaped the way I approached every challenge and opportunity that came my way. It wasn't just about overcoming obstacles; it was about setting a standard, about embodying the qualities I wished to instill in those looking up to me. "Don't miss" became not just my mantra but a principle that guided me through every decision, ensuring that every step I took was a step toward a brighter, more stable future for us all. This was the essence of our shared journey—from the depths of despair to the cusp of new beginnings—and it was a mandate to seize every moment, to fulfill every promise, and never to falter in the relentless pursuit of the future we dreamed of.

This promise, once whispered in the quiet solitude of a challenging youth, grew more profound with the arrival of my brother, mere days before I was to embark on the collegiate phase of my education. In the hospital, as I held him for the first time, feeling the delicate weight of new life in my arms, I renewed my vow with a deeper conviction.

To him, I promised to be more than just a brother; I pledged to be a beacon of reliability and a paragon of the values I hoped he would one day embody. "In your eyes, I see the future I am determined to secure for us," I vowed, feeling the stirrings of a future shaped by the choices I would make from that moment forward.

Our father's departure marked a significant fracture in our family's structure, but it was not a break in our spirit. His legacy of unkept promises and abandoned responsibilities could have cast a long shadow over our future, but instead, I filled that void with a resolute commitment to uphold the very principles he had discarded. The MICK factor—Mental resilience, Impact, Character, and the will to Keep going—transitioned from abstract ideals to the very framework of my existence. These principles, which I would later repurpose for coaching private clients, became my compass, guiding my actions and decisions with a clarity born of necessity and nurtured by determination.

"My commitment to these principles is my rebellion against the fate we were handed and my promise to deliver us a future we deserve," I often reflected, recognizing the transformative power of a steadfast resolve.

As the day of my departure for college approached, the emotional weight of years spent navigating hardship together culminated in a singular, poignant moment with my mother. She had always been a pillar of quiet strength, her resilience a silent testament to the power of enduring love. As we stood at the threshold of a new chapter, she pulled me into an embrace that seemed to compress all our years of pain, hope, and fierce love into a single, overwhelming sensation. "Don't miss," she whispered urgently into my ear, her voice a soft yet powerful command that resonated with the gravity of everything we had endured together and the boundless hope we harbored for the future.

This directive was not merely a suggestion; it was imbued with the weight of a thousand silent prayers and was as much a strategy as it was a plea. This mantra not only guided my personal endeavors but also defined my approach to leadership, emphasizing the critical importance of precision, purpose, and perseverance.

The chapter of my life detailed here is more than a retrospective glance at a difficult beginning; it is a vivid portrayal of how foundational moments can profoundly shape one's destiny. It invites readers to delve deep into the reservoirs of their own challenges, to find their *because*, and to harness the transformative power of necessity—the must-have changes that drive us toward greatness. It sets the stage for a journey of effective leadership, rooted in values and propelled by an unwavering commitment to effect meaningful change.

Thus, the narrative of my early years is more than a reflection on past sorrows; it is a vivid depiction of the moment my life's *because* was forged in the flames of hardship and hope. It sets the stage for a story of overcoming, of transforming every trial into a triumph, inviting readers to explore the depths of their own resilience, to find their *because*, and to embrace the transformative power of a must-have change.

Being an African American kid growing up in the late eighties, the only images I saw of other successful people like me were entertainers of some kind—athletes, actors, comedians, singers, and so on. Therefore, in my mind, the only way to be successful was to be the best athlete and the best student and the best person because that would get me out of my bad environment and please my mom.

So I was the kid who made straight A's; bringing home a B was a mark of failure. If I wasn't going to be the best athlete and the best leader on a sports team, I had to get straight A's to get out.

But one day, I went to this chiropractor. At my age, I didn't think it was possible for a doctor to own their practice since most doctor's offices I'd been to had been called the Something of Whatever or things like that. But this chiropractor marked the first time that I had seen someone's name on the door, and that person was also the one who helped me.

I asked him, "Are you the doctor?"

He answered, "Yes."

I asked him, "And you're also the owner?"

"Yes."

Then I asked him, "Well, what's the difference?"

He answered, "I get to write and sign the checks."

That stuck with me. At that point, I realized that the key to wealth wasn't getting the big check but being able to sign the big check. That, right there, opened up my mind to business.

When I got a scholarship to the University of North Carolina, I kept the same mentality toward my academics that I had in high school. But I also thought, *How do I become a businessperson? What do great businesspeople do?*

Channeling my mom's instructions not to miss, I networked well because I understood networking, even at eighteen years old. I knew I had to not only be with the right people but also make the biggest impact so they would remember me.

And so, in college, all my friends would tell you I was the business mind. To support my mom and the rest of my family, I had a job all through college, but I could never just be an employee—I had to be something more. My first job at a Best Buy was as a manager because naturally, I'm a leader. I am always thinking about how to prove myself in all kinds of environments, being someone who can lead people and understand the business side of things. I knew at some point that owning a business was what I wanted to do after graduating college.

Only I didn't have the funds to do that.

It was the year 2000. The internet existed, but it wasn't as widespread as it is today. Social media was not really a thing. I couldn't be a "creator" and make money, and going viral wasn't possible. You had to have money to start a serious business back then, so I did what anyone else would do: I got a job. In this case, it was a job at a nationwide insurance company. I was a sales manager.

On day one, I found myself sitting in front of one Mark Vitali. He said to me, "Mick, I want to be the biggest, baddest nationwide agent in the state of North Carolina." Those were his words, and he said we would do it in four years. I wondered how we would do this, and he told me, "That's why I hired you. You better figure this out."

And so I figured it out. I was not only the number one agent in North Carolina; we were the number one insurance agency in the country. And it was because of my principles that I could do this.

Like the chiropractor from before, Vitali was the business owner. He signed the checks and got the big bonuses, so he got to go on trips to Paris and Rome and a bunch of places in Switzerland and Canada. Meanwhile, I got to go to Atlanta, which was a big step up from where I was before.

I realized that yes, I did have a good life right now—I was accomplishing what I wanted to accomplish. But there was a bigger step, a bigger place that I was supposed to be in.

So that was when I started my own agency. Through the wisdom I learned from Vitali and the determination and grit that I always had because of the promise I made to my family, I pushed myself to success.

I became the fastest growing agent—no mergers, no acquisitions. In three years, I went to more than $3 million of revenue, which hadn't been done by a retail agent. I ended up selling the business to a large broker with six hundred employees. And then from there, I grew that company from $50 million to $70 million of revenue in four years, instilling the same principles of leadership that were bestowed upon me.

But this wasn't enough either—I wanted to show others how to do this. So I left.

Growth and leadership aren't as complicated as we make them appear. I'm not saying they're easy, but they aren't rocket science either. There's a four-letter word that's the crux of all of this: care. Care isn't something you buy. Care isn't even something you develop. Care is something that's felt, and people know when it's real and authentic. And so I made sure that was the type of leadership I had—leadership in which everyone understood that I cared. And because I cared, I was willing to do what everyone else was doing. I was willing to put things on my back. I was willing to develop and grow other leaders.

So, from a business perspective, when I talk growth strategies, I start with caring. That's why I'm now into consulting and executive coaching. I want to show people that it doesn't have to be as hard as it's made to appear. It's not easy, and there are things you have to do, but if you do them, you will gain success.

Beginning in 2016, I had a consulting business, helping insurance professionals and CEOs with growth and financial strategies. I decided to fold that into my company, Premier Strategy Box, the day before COVID-19 became an emergency. Nonetheless, Premier Strategy Box was built to help businesses hone their revenue-generating processes.

I was doing this because the insurance industry was good to me, and I felt like this was my way to give back to the field that helped develop the person I am, the person who can do the things he promised to do. But then I realized there was something further, and I was offered speaking opportunities across the country, not just in the insurance space but across other industries.

And that's where I got my first introduction to my hero, Les Brown. I saw him speak, and I knew not to miss the opportunity to pick his brain. If you're gonna shoot for the moon, don't miss. So I had a conversation with him, and he gave me his contact information.

But I wasn't quite sure what to do. I had his number, but I was not going to be the first to reach out; I wasn't sure I had the right to text or call Les Brown. But he reached out to me and said, "Hey, I've got this mastermind group that I'm forming. I'd love for you to be a part of it." And I joined his mastermind group, and that created a father-son style relationship that we still have to this day. He's the one who encouraged me to write this book. He's the one who encouraged me to get this message out there, saying, "Hey, there's no one talking about leadership the way you talk about leadership. There's no one trying to make an impact." He didn't necessarily mean in the younger generation that we were focused on, but across the board.

As he told me, John Maxwell's books are still popular, most of them were written thirty years ago, and he's not writing anything new. I felt I had to become the face of modern leadership because my mentor asked me to. But also, I have a responsibility to my family; I have children now, and my brother and sister have children of their own. I have family members and friends who look up to me. So I said to myself, "Why not put this into a manuscript? Why not make this something that can live forever?" Not only that, but I could also help people because I'm sure I'm not the only one thinking about these things. There are people in the same situation as me who are trying to figure it out, just like I had to.

We often hear that experience is the greatest teacher, but I don't think that's complete. After all, you can experience losing. In truth, it's wisdom that's the greatest teacher. The thing is that you can take the wrong lessons from experience. If you make a mistake and it turns out well, you may think you need to do it again; or when you do the right thing, but it fails as a result of circumstances outside your control, you don't do it again. You don't necessarily need experience to have wisdom. You can become an effective coach even if you haven't coached before if you've been a leader of people. And so, instead of having people lean on experience, I have them lean on wisdom.

But what is wisdom? Wisdom is the shortcut, the direction, the path that someone else has taken and can now explain to you. The most valuable thing I learned from Les is that wisdom is the best teacher, not experience. That determined why I wanted to get into executive leadership coaching—not just the consulting business but true executive leadership coaching. Because if I can provide wisdom for someone, that's what I want to do.

A useful way to think about the issue is this: If someone has many years of experience, why are they available? An organization would keep any great people unless those people were starting their own thing. Great people should never be available.

This may seem like a strange reframe, but it makes sense if you think about it: A lot of people reading this will not have experience. They'll feel this lack of experience is a knock against them, and they'll need more years of experience to be effective leaders. But by getting the wisdom, they can skip the pitfalls that experience often consists of.

My relationship with Les has provided me a lot of wisdom, and he has opened doors that I couldn't have opened on my own. Something I realized was that the principles I've been using for twenty years are the same everywhere. And when I go across the country to speak, I'm not only talking to insurance people (though I do speak at insurance industry events, too) but also speaking at multi-industry events and conferences. After I speak, a lot of people want more information, or they want a fifteen-minute call, or they want to know how to use certain innovations in their own businesses or what traits to look for in someone they might want to hire.

The purpose here is to reach more people. Only 2 percent of the world works in insurance, so I want to speak to that other 98 percent as well. And I'm doing this not for money or ego but because it's who I am.

Looking back on my childhood, I've always been the person my peers looked up to. At ten, playing on school sports teams, I would get bumped up to play alongside twelve-year-olds. Everyone centered around me, wanting me to make the decisions. Thus, I was a natural organizer of people, showing my team how best to play. Does everyone know what the goal is? Is everyone on the same page?

And it feels like the essence of good leadership is just getting everyone on the same page. When you put it like that, you find you don't need experience. You can be a good leader at ten years old.

My first client was a man named Edward "Eddie" Wright, who owned several restaurants. I was in one of his restaurants, and the owner of the restaurant group was there. I went up and introduced myself. It turned out he went to a rival college—I was from the University of North Carolina while he was from North Carolina State.

We discussed the restaurant industry—specifically, the issue of staff turnover. At first, I assumed he was hiring high school or college kids, and the turnover was so high because they were all graduating or otherwise moving on. But as I heard his explanation, I asked him something important.

"What are you providing them other than a job?"

He couldn't believe what I was saying. He said he didn't offer them anything other than a job. Then I told him he was always going to lose people because when people take on a job, they're seeking a career, so he has to provide something more than the job itself.

Thus, we went through his whole process. We bolstered his training and onboarding. We went into pathways to promotion: for example, going from cashier to general manager. And once you're a general manager, there's a path to getting equity. And so it was doing these things that changed his business and his revenue and made him a better leader because, at that moment, he saw that it wasn't just about a job.

Eddie then asked me how I could help transform his business. The usual practice was to just hire people for specific jobs in order to replace employees who left, but Eddie wanted to do better. So I suggested that I come in, redefine his company culture from day one, and build a career path for people, starting with a clean slate. We even junked the old mission and vision statements. However, I made it clear that he was the leader of the company; I was never going to give him something that was my idea that he couldn't implement on his own. I also told him if he could have these conversations and work with me for six months, I promised he would have a better culture in his company and retain more of his employees. He told me if I could do that, he'd hire me for life.

Thus, he's been a client of mine for three years straight.

My next client was a woman named Rebecca at a health-care company. I met her at a convention, and when I talked to her, I learned that we grew up within a couple of hundred miles of each other. Coming back to the present, she was struggling with how to become an effective leader because health care is hard. How could she get her team better? Everyone was licensed, so she had people who met the qualifications, but how do you have efficiency in staffing? How do you have efficiency in your business? How do you care about the well-being of your staff? Rebecca worked in an emergency room, so she saw the most horrific things every day.

I told her that ER staff are trained for these horrific things, but you can't make those the things that they do. She asked me what I meant, and I told her that if someone comes in with a heart attack, a stroke, or injuries from an electric shock, her team is there. What's the plan when something goes wrong? Her team isn't the doctor, and most situations in emergency rooms do not end well. The question here was how Rebecca could mentally prepare her staff to handle all these tragedies every single day; she had never thought about that.

So with my help, she implemented a lot of mental health training for these medical professionals, as well as some around business strategy. But for Rebecca, it was about teaching her how to not just be the face of a unit but the leader who cared for her team, understanding the toll the job took on them. She had focused on running the ER unit and not enough on what exactly went on in these situations. There's a lot of training around leadership hospitals do, but it's easier said than done when you actually have to live it, lead it, and teach it.

I've been doing executive leadership coaching full time for four years now, and before that, I was an insurance consultant for ten years. That's a lot of time and a lot of wisdom. And now, it's time for me to share that wisdom with you, so you can become not just a great leader but, more importantly, a good one.

1

Great Leaders Aren't *Good* Leaders?

Imagine you're leading a meeting.

Everyone is looking at you, waiting for you to provide direction. But inside, you feel lost and unprepared. Your heart races, your palms sweat, and the awkward silence becomes deafening. In the few seconds that follow, you start to question your abilities. You wonder if you're cut out for this role. What if your superiors made a huge mistake in offering you this position? What if *you* made a huge mistake in accepting it?

What if I told you that this experience is more common than you think—and that even the greatest leaders have felt this way?

Perhaps you've never had a role model to look to as an example of how to lead effectively. Now you find yourself struggling to connect with your team, let alone drive any meaningful change.

Many young leaders face the challenge of navigating their careers without the benefit of seasoned guidance. They feel overwhelmed by the expectations placed on them, and resources on how to develop the necessary skills to lead confidently aren't easy to find. New leaders today face unprecedented challenges. The fast-paced, ever-changing business landscape asks leaders to adapt quickly and secure buy-in from their teams, all while driving innovation. Without the right guidance, many leaders find themselves stuck, unable to progress, and facing high levels of stress and burnout. The pressures of leadership are real and relentless, and without a clear framework of support, the risk of failure is high.

I wrote this book to address these critical issues. My goal is to provide you with a framework that helps you not only survive but also *thrive* as a leader.

This book is for both aspiring and imminent leaders. If that's you, you might feel like your job is primarily a negative one—don't embarrass yourself, don't get demoted, don't fail your organization, avoid public humiliation, or all of the above. So what old and trusted tool do you have to get this job done?

Examples you've seen of others in positions of leadership have most likely subsisted of either aggression or abdication—or an oscillation between both. Either the leader tries to make people obey, or they set no expectations at all and are nowhere to be found when clarification or support is needed. Maybe the leader issues threats regarding underperformance or noncompliance, but fails to enforce them when the time comes. Or, they act lax on the rules at the outset, but come down with a hammer when it's least expected.

None of this is great leadership. It's not *good* either. There's a difference between these, by the way, which is probably the missing piece of the leadership puzzle you're now tasked with assembling. The focus on greatness is a focus on self-validation. The focus on goodness is one grown from others. Meaning, the aspiring great leader looks to the praise (or the criticism) of followers and peers to gauge whether or not they are doing a good job. And they equate their worth as leaders—according to third parties—with their self-worth. Thus, the ego gets brittle. Any little change to their authority becomes an existential threat. There is no room for negotiation or nuance, and everyone must walk on eggshells. Perhaps you know of such a leader or have worked for one (or many!). Contrast this with the good leader, who is focused not on validation but impact. Are their employees, students, or anyone else they're responsible for doing better than before? Making fewer mistakes and fixing those mistakes they do make? That is what good leaders inspire. They are all but ego-free. It's not about self; it's about service. It sounds cliché, but that's just the way it is.

And it can feel very challenging, risky, and even scary to put yourself out there and try to be that kind of leader. Whether you want to be great or better yet, good, whatever your aspiration, you probably do not yet know exactly what that future leader you looks like, sounds like, or leads like. Challenging, risky, and scary indeed.

So what do you do with all this negativity? When your palms are sweating and your thoughts are racing, I'm going to show you how to use that fear—and harness it to *win*. Win over your team, win the trust of your colleagues, and win back your confidence in your own abilities as a leader.

When you've finished reading this book, you'll have the transformative framework you need to become not just a good leader, but an exceptional one. Even if you've never had a mentor or role model to look up to, even if you feel lost, discouraged, and burned out, you'll walk away from this book with the tools to foster innovation, encourage creativity, and persevere through challenges. This book will lift the weight off your shoulders and keep your feet on the ground. It will empower you to lead with confidence, inspire your team, and make a significant impact in your organization and beyond.

My Clients

How can I be so sure? Because coaching new or aspiring leaders like you is what I do for a living.

Darren Vermost

My client, Darren Vermost, owner of Vermost Insurance Agency, was facing significant challenges when I met him. His team cohesion was lacking (meaning no one was working together the way they should have been), and it was causing inconsistent performance across the company. Darren's initial efforts had been focused on implementing traditional sales and marketing strategies, but these methods focused on singling out individual performance metrics. As you might imagine, this was leading to low morale and high turnover rates.

As his executive coach, I introduced Darren to the principles outlined in this book. We worked on his mental resilience, and shifted our focus toward building a supportive team culture. By conducting workshops on imagination and innovation, we encouraged creative problem-solving and collaboration within his team. We implemented a system for recognizing and celebrating small wins, which boosted everyone's morale.

Through our coaching sessions, Darren transformed his leadership style, resulting in a 30 percent increase in team productivity. This transformation highlights the power of the principles in this book. By fostering a culture of creativity and courage, a cohesive and motivated team emerged, and performance naturally increased.

Chris Paradiso

Another client of mine, Chris Paradiso, owner of Paradiso Insurance, struggled with low client engagement. This was despite some pretty heavy investments in digital marketing and social media. His approach was too broad and his content fell flat, which failed to create any strong connections with potential clients.

During our coaching sessions, I helped Chris refine his marketing strategy by focusing on personalized storytelling and client-specific messages. We trained his team on effective storytelling techniques to enhance client interactions and build stronger relationships. Then we introduced a feedback loop to continuously gather and incorporate his clients' insights into his future marketing efforts.

As a result, Chris saw a 25 percent increase in client engagement and improved support from his team. Chris's success demonstrates the transformative impact of targeted communication and storytelling, proving that personalized marketing strategies can significantly enhance client relationships—and, therefore, sales.

Madison Glover

Madison Glover, owner of Pinnacle Marketing Solutions, was seeing inconsistent revenue streams and a high client turnover. Madison's previous strategies focused on short-term gains, which led to a lack of sustained growth and very few long-term client relationships.

Through our executive coaching sessions, Madison applied the innovative and resilient leadership techniques from this book.

We shifted her focus toward long-term client relationship management and retention strategies. By developing a strong, purpose-driven brand narrative through *because* statements (more on this later), Madison's marketing campaigns resonated deeply with clients, making a larger impact on revenue.

In fact, within six months, Madison achieved a remarkable 40 percent growth in her business. This success demonstrates the effectiveness of developing long-term client relationships for sustained business success.

Eddie Wright

My client Eddie Wright, owner of Summit Hospitality Group, struggled with consistent customer satisfaction and employee turnover. This was despite his significant investments in high-end staff training. Eddie's focus on operational efficiency overlooked the crucial aspects of employee satisfaction and engagement. This directly affected his customers' experiences.

I guided Eddie in fostering a culture of innovation and continuous improvement. We implemented employee recognition programs and regular feedback sessions to boost morale and align the team with the company's vision. We also developed customer-centric training programs to enhance the overall customer experience.

After working with me, Eddie launched three new projects that led to a 20 percent increase in revenue. His new strategic leadership drove business growth and created a culture of continuous improvement.

Rebecca Williams

My client Rebecca Williams, a health-care leader at Horizon Health Services, was failing in project delivery. Her staff morale was down, despite providing an array of patient care initiatives and training programs for her team. Her focus on clinical excellence alone led to a disconnect between business efficiency and staff well-being.

Rebecca adopted this book's principles, increasing her mental resilience and strategic thinking. We developed stress management techniques for the staff. We introduced a continuous feedback system to streamline project delivery and align clinical and operational goals.

As a result, Rebecca improved project delivery times by 35 percent, showcasing the significant impact of mental resilience on operational success. This transformation highlights the importance of a holistic approach to leadership, emphasizing both clinical excellence and operational efficiency.

There are many more stories where these come from, which you can find on my website, mickunplugged.com. I'm confident this book will enable you to experience results like these as a leader, whether you've been in your position for a while or you're still dreaming of stepping into it.

This book is so like my coaching and so unlike other available books on leadership.

If you go to your local bookstore and pick up a book that's supposed to teach you how to be a great leader, you'd probably feel like you're chasing a train that's leaving the station. The conductor continues to wave you up, encouraging you to jump aboard. But no matter how fast you run, the train just gets farther and farther away. No matter how far you read, tangible advice that you can implement today is harder and harder to find.

To lead well, you need a growth mindset. To have a growth mindset, you need to be confident in your abilities. To be confident, you need to communicate effectively. Each piece of advice in other leadership books is built on a separate piece of advice that's only partially explained. You're chasing something that feels important, yet the farther you get, the more confused and overwhelmed you become.

These books often contain stories of highly publicized people in high-stakes situations. These stories detail what they did, followed by the author's commentary amounting to, "Yeah, so just do that." But there's no obvious similarity between your situation and that of the famous person. If you compare Theodore Roosevelt's invasion to getting a project done by the weekend, does that mean you should threaten to fire everyone if they don't comply? This leads to taking the wrong lessons from the wrong stories, forcing you, the reader, to search for a voice in your head to tell you what to do, not finding that voice, and being stuck with uncertainty. But what would Roosevelt do? I have no idea. Or maybe, what would Steve Jobs do?

These are entirely the wrong questions, and asking them sends your goals even further away. This book will show you what to ask instead. As you dive in, you'll not only see your goals more clearly than you ever have before, you'll have concrete directions on how to both achieve and sustain them.

Without the overwhelm and burn out weighing you down, you'll even feel excited as you take the next steps on your leadership journey.

Remember at the beginning of this chapter when I asked you to imagine you were leading a meeting? Let's find out what happens when you can finally relax into your position and lead your team with confidence. Because to be frank, the alternative to you embodying the good leadership of this book is pretty gnarly.

For some, good leadership doesn't feel like enough. The perception of greatness—of being considered great by others—is a real temptation, especially for people who are self-conscious. I get it. In the past, I've tied my sense of self to what others said about me and thought about me (or really, what I thought they would be thinking). I got lost in my own hallucinations of what I imagined were very real feelings other people had toward me, and I would simulate over and over how I would, could, and should react to them to "tell them off" or to "show them." What was I not doing all the while? Serving. Supporting. Motivating. Which is what good leaders do. By worrying about not being considered great, I became not good.

The first time I assumed a leadership position, I found myself responsible for three hundred people. All eyes were on me. And so I thought it was about me. All about me. I thought I was literally supposed to lead three hundred individuals, individually. I learned pretty quickly that logistically speaking, that's not possible. There is not enough time in the day to manage every aspect of three hundred people's performance individually myself. Furthermore, to try to manage their opinion of me was even harder. That is the way to burnout.

And so I realized soon into the job that my job as a leader wasn't to lead people in a "tell each of you what to do" sense; my job as a leader was to lead everyone to become capable leaders of others. To empower and to equip them so I would not have to be a control freak in chief. And so I made a choice:

I decided to be a good leader.

With this book, you have been given that same choice.

What will you choose?

••••

After you finish *How to Be a Good Leader When You've Never Had One*, I'd love to continue your leadership journey with you. That's why I'm inviting you to join the Mick Unplugged Community. This community is more than just a network—it's a comprehensive resource for ongoing growth and development.

By joining the Mick Unplugged Community, leaders like you will gain access to:

- **The MICK Factor Leadership Assessment:** This exclusive assessment will help you identify your strengths and areas for improvement within my private coaching framework, which I call the MICK Factor. It's a personalized tool that provides insights into your leadership style and offers tailored strategies you can implement for growth.
- **Business Assessments:** In addition to the leadership assessment, you'll have access to other assessments focused on sales, mindset, and more. These assessments are designed to provide a holistic view of your professional capabilities and areas for development.
- **VIP Content Access:** Members of the Mick Unplugged Community will receive VIP access to exclusive content that I put out. This includes webinars, workshops, and other educational resources that aren't available to the general public. You'll be the first to know about new insights and strategies that can propel your leadership and business forward.
- **Discounts on Masterminds and Summits:** As a member, you'll enjoy special discounts on all Masterminds and Summits hosted by Mick Unplugged. These events are powerful opportunities for intensive learning, networking, and personal growth. By attending, you'll be able to dive deeper into the principles discussed in the book and apply them in a collaborative and supportive environment.

Joining the Mick Unplugged Community makes it effortless to commit to continuous improvement and excellence in leadership. It's a space where you'll find like-minded professionals who are equally dedicated to becoming the best leaders they can be. Together, we'll explore new ideas, challenge each other, and grow in ways we never thought possible.

Go to community.mickunplugged.com to join.

2

False Aspirations: Why You Don't Want to Be a "Great" Leader

Have you ever watched those viral motivational videos? There's an epic soundtrack, clips from beloved movies so well-known that most of us can recite the lines from memory, all interspersed with stock photography of the sort of people and situations many of us can relate to. For example, if you suddenly find yourself in anything like a leadership position and you watch a motivational video on the subject, you might find a role model in motion picture protagonists who raise their voices (and fists), use lots of exciting nonverbals to get their point across, whip out every inspirational cliché we already know, and tell everyone what to do.

This person is the boss, and everyone in the clip has to fall in line—be they athletes on a sports team, soldiers or sailors or aviators in an armed force, students in a classroom, or sales reps in a cubicle farm. And in these motivational clips, they do fall in line. The top dog calls the shots, and all the good little people obey at once, without question. There is a crescendo of enthusiasm toward the close of these videos that pumps you up so much you have to jump up and do likewise.

Except it doesn't work.

Even worse, this leadership style—if you can even call it that—doesn't just *not* work for you, it works *against* you. Speak like the heroes or heroines in these movies and shows and speeches, and you'll turn away people who would otherwise have followed your lead. Now your job is that much harder because you live action role-played as Denzel, and you were not convincing in the slightest. That's not leadership; and yet, that's the best model most of us have.

Leadership Versus Influence

Is there a place for inspirational messages, even those that drive motivation into us then drive us out into the world to make things happen? For sure, but don't call that leadership. That's being an influencer of opinion. It's not leading. It's not guiding individuals who may become leaders in their own right. Rah-rah soundtracks and scenes and clips and excitement are influence.

Which brings us to the difference between the concepts of hard power and soft power. Hard power is hierarchy and authority; for example, the US military has plenty of hard power, as does the Internal Revenue Service. Cross either organization, and you will have a bad time. But soft power is more like the social media influencer, opinion-shaper, or sense-maker. It's the analyst on your favorite news channel, account, or profile. Soft power is your favorite social account follow. It's your mom. These individuals may not have literal power over you, but many have the capacity and ability to shape how you think, what you feel, and so on. That's soft power.

Motivational leadership videos are also soft power, even those that come across as pretty hardcore. But inside an organization, be it a church, an office, a school, or another such situation, you, as the leader, have hard power over those you're responsible for, with them being accountable to you. You need much less soft power to move them to do as you say because their default answer is already yes—after all, you're the boss.

So if you try to exercise too much soft power, you look as though you're trying hard because you must. You look as if you lack hard power. You look like an impostor. Like you're not really the boss because, if you were, you wouldn't try to act like Will Smith, Russell Crowe, and Sylvester Stallone all in one, would you?

So that brings us to the paradox of humble power. You hold your people in the palm of your hand, so you don't need to squeeze them. A good boss, then, doesn't have to act like a great one.

Don't Be a Try-hard

If you're tracking with me, you may have already changed your mind a little bit or at least adjusted your thoughts now. Perhaps before, you thought that an effective leader needs to command the room with great charisma. You may not think that now. You might be realizing that your title is enough to warrant a minimum viable level of influence; this is good.

What you do with that matters, and you realize now that being a try-hard burns away the respect you walk into a room with.

That over-the-top approach may even cause employees to undermine you because you seem to be acting as if there's a real boss somewhere who isn't you; you're merely the annoying cheerleader for whoever is really calling the shots.

So let's take a different approach—that of humble power, when your people listen to you because they want to. Hard and soft power, in perfect balance. *OK, I'm following you, Mick. But what does that look like?*

I'm glad you asked. But I won't tell you. I'll show you.

Darren: Leading in the Gray

I spoke with an insurance agency owner named Darren. He was the leader, and everyone looked up to him. His view of leadership was "the buck stops with me"—he made all the decisions, and he was the driving force, the hard power who kept everyone in line. Thanks to his military background, he was convincing in the role. His team would do anything for him, to the point of being a little afraid of him.

So the very first thing I did with Darren was go through emotional intelligence; he had to connect with his team emotionally. Yes, everyone knows you're the leader, but do they know you as a person? So we worked on his soft skills. We considered how he was communicating with the team, and we had him overthink every communication. Before he hit send, before he scheduled a meeting, he had to consider where he was at mentally. He had to change how he communicated with his team.

To do this, he had to appear softer than he was. He had to recognize that his team didn't share his military background or his educational accomplishments, so he had to change the atmosphere he created. That meant working with Darren to change the workplace culture and build it back up the right way. And that's what turned things around. Once the culture was brought up to speed, it became easier for me to coach him.

His main issue was that he was very black and white—a blunt person who didn't want to fluff up anything. He always went straight to the point. But when you're leading, you can't be that way all of the time; you have to have emotional intelligence, which means you have to understand who you're surrounded with. He had to tap into all ranges of emotions and soft skills; he had to make his people follow him because they wanted to, not because they had to. But a balance had to be struck, too—if he tried too hard to make them want to follow him, then they'd feel they no longer had to follow him.

There's also a difference between motivation and inspiration. You don't want to get your team motivated to come to work—that's on them. You want them to be inspired. The main motivation to work is money, so if that's all you have, your team will leave the moment someone offers more money for the same work. But if all else is equal, or even if you pay a little less but they're inspired to come work for you, that's the difference between good and great. You want to be good by inspiring people to come in.

The result? Morale increased dramatically.

But how did we know this? Simple—because Darren could focus on being a CEO. He didn't have to wear every hat like before because now, the team was inspired to take those hats themselves. He didn't have to be the office manager; he let his existing office manager do the job instead. People enhanced their individual skills and their productivity. And so Darren was a good leader.

Chris: Leading While Young

Chris is not only a client but, like Darren, also one of my best friends in life. He's the guy who will try anything and everything. He has shiny-object syndrome: if there's a new tech product, Chris goes straight for it. If there's some new digital or social platform, Chris is on it.

But Chris's problem was that his customers didn't engage. He was doing all these cool things but getting no buy-in from customers. If customers aren't engaging, then the team is inadequate, which meant Chris's leadership was inadequate. As the company owner, Chris rarely sees clients, but his team does. So Chris shouldn't have been upset about low client engagement but about the fact that he wasn't connecting with his team. His team builds the strong relationships and talks to the clients. They're the ones responding to emails and doing all the communication. So how could Chris connect better with his team?

He had to get in tune with how the modern employee works, since his staff was a generation younger than he was. Even though Chris is tech savvy, his communication was not. To get the team on his side, Chris had to state goals and inspire them to understand where he wanted them to go. He had to explain his vision—a skill all good leaders should have.

As he moved away from his old communication habits and adopted newer, better ones, the team's performance improved. They took ownership of those client touchpoints and made use of the technology he was bringing on board. Now, he not only gets client engagement but also gets to play around with his tech more. The clients engage with the technology, and Chris connects with people better.

How so? I can illustrate this with a story.

Chris lives in Stafford Springs, Connecticut. He does a big event on Flag Day that the whole town turns out for. In fact, for the past seven years, Flag Day has been like Christmas in Stafford Springs. But the pinnacle came when the community rallied around Chris and all the things he was doing because the community was his client. Flag Day went from 200 people to 2,500 people. Thus, he not only got more involved with his team, but he also got more involved with his community as a whole. He became a good leader.

Madison: Leading from **Because**

Madison had extremely high turnover in what she was doing. She thought of great leadership as keeping the numbers in front of her. It was all about hitting targets and goals with her. Everything was about the goal—you gotta do this; you gotta do that. It was a rigid way of thinking.

One of the major things we did with Madison was get away from the corporate mission and vision statements. I could guess those mission and vision statements after reading five words of them. I don't care what business it is or what industry it is—I can figure it out. So I told Madison that her team didn't know any of this, but I had to show her.

I pulled the team into the room and asked them if they could recite the mission and vision statements. Less than 5 percent of that room raised their hands. After I showed Madison this, I told her that her team needed to understand why she did what she did. Why was she there? She's not the owner of the company. I asked her what got her out of bed every morning. Why did she want to be here? Why did she want to lead this team?

She said some platitudes, and that was it. I answered that if her team didn't understand the reason behind the reason for what she did and she couldn't list it in three bullet points, her team would never believe in her.

I had her build *because* statements because Madison's team needed to understand why she came to work. But the *because* statement for the department wasn't for her; it was for the team and for the clients she hoped to attract. Once the team understood Madison's *because*, they did that for themselves, too. Then we built a committee that rebuilt the *because* statements for Madison's department, which then became the *because* statements for the company. And all this gave the team a sense of purpose. They knew why they were doing it, and where they were going. And, more importantly, everyone could communicate that clearly with clients and prospects.

And so the aha moment for the group was they understood Madison and her push because they understood the reason she was authoritative about her goals. But if they didn't know of her struggles—of being a single mother and getting ready for kids who are off to college—she would just come off as a dictator being mean for the sake of being mean. They understood her reasons, which they could rally behind. It also helped them build purposeful *because* statements and gave them a reason to keep moving forward. And the result was growth, low client turnover, and low employee turnover, too. All things considered, Madison's change was a success. She became a good leader.

Rebecca: Leading Without Distractions

Rebecca had low morale on her team. She worked in a hospital, and nobody was hitting their numbers. Despite being good at the job, Rebecca didn't feel like a leader, though her skills got her promoted to a position of authority. But being good at something doesn't necessarily qualify you for a leadership role. And that was it—she felt unqualified for the role, so she wanted to go back to being a mere team member.

So when Rebecca and I spoke, we talked about the mental resilience she would need for her job. But, more importantly, she had to think strategically. How could she take a situation or project and plan things out instead of diving straight into it? How would she put people in the right places in the project to do the things she needed them to do? Among the challenges of the healthcare industry are stress management and time management, so we focused on squaring those away, too.

Rebecca understood that being a good leader wasn't about the things she did to get there but about pushing her team to move forward and having them follow her because they wanted to. If you're a skilled basketball player who can score fifty points any time you want, it's not good enough that you alone can do that. You're going to have better success when five other people on your team can do the same thing.

That meant that she couldn't jump on the phone every time someone called. She didn't have to be the best at everything. Once she realized that, she gave her teammates a chance to shine. And now, her team is winning awards. Within the health-services community, people on her team were getting asked to speak in places, people on her team were getting calls to collaborate with other systems, and things like that.

Before, she wasn't planning things in advance, and she wasn't exercising her hard power as the boss. But now, she feels like a great leader. She has become more flexible in her methods, responding to things as they come up. By using her hard power, she now has soft power. She is now a good leader.

Rolling It All Up into Good Leadership

I want you to imagine a leader who embodies all these admirable traits—a Darren, a Chris, a Madison, and a Rebecca, all rolled into one. You wouldn't need them to be a hyperactive, loud motivator to follow them into battle and beyond. You would just do it because of who they are. Yes, they are the boss, but you trust them implicitly to be a *good* boss. There is no doubt in your mind that they will do the right thing, and if they make a bad decision, they will do everything to set it right. It's the perfect balance of hard and soft power. That's what *good* leadership looks like.

Now let's imagine the opposite; it's not hard. It's all too easy to fall into the trap of becoming just that—a leader who is, without irony and not as a joke, *bad at leading*.

3

The Six Traits of "Great" Leaders Who Aren't *Good* Leaders

Great business minds often make for terrible leadership. This is because the fundamental joint activities of business success are marketing and sales—that is, persuading and winning, convincing and converting. The best in the business—in any business—are master marketers and salespeople.

You know that silly challenge to "sell me this pen"? These guys and gals can actually pull that off; you want to buy the pen when they're done. Now it's your pen.

But all life is trade-offs. There are pros for every con and vice versa. The thing about good persuasion is that you know how to semi-ethically exaggerate the benefits of a product while downplaying known disadvantages, downsides, or doubts. So long as you can offer convinced customers technical support should your hyperbolic pitch for your product not pan out—so long as you make good on any overpromising to people who buy from you so they leave satisfied—this is all strength.

There is an obvious concern with overpromising and underdelivering, of course. And that is exactly what many of the world's best businesspeople do when they become business leaders. They sell themselves on their exaggerated people-building and team-managing abilities. They market themselves on traits they don't really have that would qualify them for the job. It's not good for anyone; least of all the business leader.

You may have a great businessperson who, upon accepting the responsibility to lead others, becomes inexplicably terrible at the job. But is it unexplainable, or is it what we might expect from such a person? I think it is what we could expect, and in this chapter, I'll walk you through the six traits I have seen on a recurring basis in my more than twenty years in business. The greatest irony of all is that not-so-great leaders believe these qualities to be helpful. They are not.

Even if you are not the sort of motivational try-hard we discussed (and dismissed!) in Chapter 2, there are other, less obvious and more insidious traits of poor leadership that even the best of us fall into practicing, with the mistaken belief that it's just what good leaders do. It's not. By knowing these trait traps, you can avoid them or recover if you've already fallen into them.

Six Ways to Lead Poorly

Bad leaders self-deceive.

They disguise micromanagement as attention to detail and see a dictatorial approach as "strong leadership." They pretend to delegate tasks, supposedly allowing their subordinates to do a task however they please, but in truth, they're telling the subordinates exactly how to do things. They also lack empathy and play at being tough. I know, because I worked under a leader like that once.

But we can sniff out this self-deception.

Let's say I just met a client who I'm coaching in leadership. I'll not only ask them what their *why* is, but also why it is their *why*.

And then, they'll say something like they're doing this for their kids or to make money or to help out wherever it is they are. But when I ask why that's their *why*, they can't answer in the exact same way. No one's going to say, "Creating profit is my *why*"—there needs to be a *because* attached to it.

Bad leaders take themselves at face value. They take their own surface-level explanations as the accurate description of reality. Or they take their self-deceit as some kind of insight into what's going on. They have ideas of what good traits are, but they're wrong.

Bad Leaders Self-deceive

Let's explain.

- **Trait perceived as good:** I have confidence in myself, so I trust my instincts.
- **Actual impact:** The poor leader believes their own hype, so they forget they're deceiving themselves. They're wrong about things, and they're confident about those wrong things.

For example, take that boss I mentioned before. I asked him his motivation, and he said that his motivation was to make money.

I wanted to know *why* he wanted to make money, yet he just kept going back to money. Eventually, he admitted that he wanted awards and recognition. Then I asked him if his team knew that—if he'd told them, specifically, that this was his motivation. Because if he hadn't, he'd come across as ego driven. He had hidden the real reason from himself, but all it took was a couple of questions to get the truth out of him.

Bad Leaders Disguise Micromanagement as Attention to Detail

> **Trait perceived as good:** A keen eye for detail to ensure high standards are met.
> **Actual impact:** Micromanagement stifles team creativity, reduces employee autonomy, and creates an environment of mistrust. It demotivates team members and hampers their professional growth, leading to high turnover rates and decreased productivity.

Haley is an insurance agency owner, and she is the epitome of this management style. She has a checklist for everything and sees herself as having great attention to detail. She thinks she's running a tight ship, making sure everything stays on track.

In truth, she is making her well-paid employees look as if they're doing a minimum-wage task because, when everything's a checklist, you're taking the humanity out of it all. What ends up happening is that the team cares more about getting the checklist right than doing the job they're actually supposed to be doing.

Thus I told Haley that the checklists had to go.

Of course, she objected, saying that without the checklists, people would label things wrong. I told Haley that while she created a company that's great at auditing and she herself is good at her job, she also created a culture of fear that if someone doesn't get something done, if the checklist isn't completed, or if an employee scores low on an audit, people's jobs are on the line. What matters more is that they're taking care of your customers and growing your business. It's not about the checklist because that's not leadership. You hired people to do the job because you trusted that they'd do it right; you did not set out to make bad hires. If you did make bad hires, point to those people, not everyone as a whole.

So here's how I explained it to Haley: a better way to do things is to have a manual of standard operating procedures that people can always reference. That said, the process you want the employees to follow should have no more than seven steps; the moment you go above seven, it'll feel like a checklist. You want to say things like "When you do this, these are the seven things you want to make sure you're doing." But make it feel like a flow, not a list. Be like "Do this first, then do this, then go here, then go over here, then come back here." That's better than "You gotta do this, then you gotta attach that, label it this way," and so on. People should know that it doesn't have to be written out. Five to seven things are easy to remember, while sixty to seventy things are downright impossible. Following procedure should be intuitive.

Bad Leaders Perceive Dictatorship to Be Strong Leadership

- **Trait perceived as good:** Strong and decisive leadership that ensures control and order.
- **Actual impact:** A dictatorial style alienates team members, fosters a culture of fear, and discourages open communication. It suppresses team input and collaboration, leading to a lack of diverse ideas and innovative solutions.

Peter's worst trait was his "my way or the highway" tendency. He made every decision and wanted to be recognized for making those decisions. For example, he was choosing a new software vendor, and he wanted the least expensive option he could find. It didn't suit the company well, but Peter had already made up his mind, so the company had to use the software he chose. This led to two years of the company wrestling with awful software. Even so, Peter insisted on making all the decisions regarding software acquisition.

He was never going to talk to a customer. He was never going to sell a policy. He was never going to file a claim. He was never going to change a vehicle on the platform. But he made every decision as if he was. And so, it led to chaos, confusion, and ultimately turnover because people left.

The idea here is that Peter had made the decision already. While it's well within a leader's rights to make decisions, good leaders allow decisions to be altered as needed with new information. Dictators, by contrast, ignore new information that could affect past decisions or alter future ones. This does not mean abdicating the leadership role and trying to run the company as a democracy. It's more like holding court and accepting the wisdom of your royal council.

That said, you can still make the hard call, the unpopular but necessary decision. You can even act as the dictator if you consistently make good decisions, though that's a massive risk. The point is that, as boss, you have the hard power, and hard power is necessary. But you also need soft power so your advisors and even your employees can trust your judgment in making crucial decisions.

Bad Leaders Self-promote Under the Guise of "Inspirational Leadership"

Trait perceived as good: Demonstrating personal achievements to inspire and motivate the team.

Actual impact: Self-promotion creates an environment in which the leader's achievements overshadow the team's contributions. This can breed resentment, reduce team cohesion, and demotivate employees who feel their efforts are not recognized or valued.

A leader who reported to me—let's call her Tina—always loved to highlight every great thing she did for me. She went ahead and did a report for me, then let me know it, so I knew it was done under her direction. I took her work and fixed it up; it was pretty good.

At first, this appears to be someone taking the initiative, showing others how they too can do well in the company. However, Tina wasn't doing this to encourage others but to boost herself. She didn't want someone else to win the award; she wanted it for herself.

Likewise, Ian would always brag about the business deals he put together ten to fifteen years ago. He would name drop significant people like Steve Jobs or Steve Forbes, along with anyone else he had solved problems for.

That blatant self-promotion sounds inspirational, but Ian always focused on the fact that he had lunch with Steve Jobs. His bragging about his importance was obvious to everyone except the person telling the story because of the incredible amount of self-deception it takes to act like that. Ian wasn't trying to inspire. He was trying to flex.

I also had this conversation with someone on my team at Strategy Box when that person got a follow-back from some low-level celebrity, then started bragging about how he got it from regularly putting up content and tagging the right people.

But here's the problem: that person wasn't inviting him places. That person didn't ask for contact information. That person didn't engage at all; all he got was a pat on the back. He likely tagged five thousand people and got one of them to follow him back, but it stopped at a follow.

The problem with all this is that it's focused on polishing one person's ego, not doing anything to help the team. It's more about taking than giving, even if the only thing being taken is attention. Someone full of themselves who gives nothing back is not good for the group at all.

Bad Leaders Over-delegate and Call It "Empowerment"

Trait perceived as good: Delegating tasks to empower and trust the team.

Actual impact: Over-delegation can result in a lack of clear direction and support for team members. It may lead to confusion, inadequate resources for task completion, and a perception of the leader as disengaged or unwilling to contribute.

Delegation is taking something off your plate and assigning it to someone else. Leaders are always told to delegate so they have more time for other tasks. However, if all you do is delegate, you reduce your level of responsibility. You become more like a manager than a leader.

In the book *The E-Myth* by Michael Gerber, you learn that entrepreneurs work *on* the business, not *in* the business; thus, leaders do have to delegate when necessary. However, there can be too much of a good thing. When you hand off tasks to someone else, it's as if you're taking no responsibility for them because the person you handed them off to is skilled at them. Someone I work closely with—let's call her Cora—took an idea she was supposed to run with and handed it to someone else. It was like she was trying to feed this other person things to do instead of taking some responsibility for how the job was completed.

But how do we draw the line between over-delegating and under-delegating?

Under-delegating is wearing all the hats. It's acting like a control freak, saying you've got to see everything, you've got to review everything, and you have to hold on to something so you can finish it properly. By contrast, over-delegating is when you're just telling everyone what to do because you think that's how a great leader should act. You think you're empowering people by telling them exactly what to do everywhere and in every way, but you're not.

Cora was in a strategy meeting with me once. We were discussing how we were going to add automation packages. I asked her to help me think about ways we could use automation, but she handed that responsibility over to Harold. Instead of inviting Harold to come in and brainstorm together or have a discussion, she outsourced the mind mapping to Harold, not even bothering to be the middleman. If I wanted a conversation with Harold, I would have done that, but I wanted a conversation with Cora. I wanted to hear her thoughts, not someone else's.

It matters how the news is received by the employee. Is it received as collaboration and empowerment or just having to bear more weight, especially if the thing being assigned isn't their regular job? Only delegate when the person you're giving the job to has that area of responsibility in most cases.

Just as delegating too much is bad, handing jobs to the wrong people is bad. Ensure that you have enough rapport with your subordinates that they feel comfortable telling you if what you've given them to do isn't in their area of expertise. Actual empowerment means that those under you can resist being given too many tasks or the wrong tasks. They are empowered when they tell you that because they're not responsible for one area of the business, they have no stake in it, but someone else is the right fit. This is not being insubordinate or difficult but trying to redirect tasks toward whoever can best do them. But if someone is resisting an appropriately delegated task, then you know you have a difficult employee.

Also, keep in mind that over-delegating is not letting someone have control either. It overlaps with giving your employees a checklist by taking control away from them. Trust them to do their jobs correctly.

Bad Leaders Lack Empathy and Pretend to Be Tough

> **Trait perceived as good:** Maintaining a professional distance to ensure objectivity and fairness.
> **Actual impact:** A lack of empathy results in poor interpersonal relationships, diminished team morale, and an unsupportive work environment. Employees feel undervalued and disconnected, which can reduce overall engagement in and loyalty to the organization.

Lack of empathy is most painful when an employee has a need. Let's say the employee's kids are sick, and that employee needs some time off. The boss then answers by saying that a project is due in five days, then blames the employee for not getting it done despite the difficult situation at home. This is a more common scenario than you might think.

Another scenario is an annual performance review. It's easy to give a good one, but when it's time to give a bad one, that's when a lack of empathy can show. Are you being tough because you'll have to say no to a raise or a promotion? So then you act like a movie character, talking tough and going straight to the facts to prove a point about how much you don't care? This is when the lack of empathy is seen and felt the most.

Let's consider a scenario: Mr. Jones is on the line, and he's got a sad situation. The employee feels like there's something they should do more of, or the employee feels they need to get someone else involved. So that's the employee coming to you.

You say, "Hey, it's your customer. You know what to do—go handle it." The employee came to you seeking help, only for you to tell them to go handle it.

By contrast, empathy would be feeling that the employee is coming to you as the boss, saying they need help with a customer. This employee feels overwhelmed. Perhaps they feel the customer's escalation is beyond what they're capable of handling. They feel like they're in need of help, and they feel you're trustworthy enough so they come to you, only for you to prove them wrong.

That's not being tough. That's being a coward.

This is because an employee came to you with a difficult situation, but you ducked out in response. You're supposed to be able to handle tougher situations than your employees can handle. And now you're turning back around to your employee and telling them to handle a tough situation, all because you don't want to help.

A better way to answer is like so: talk to the employee about the situation, then ask that employee how they would respond. You're just talking things out, giving them the confidence to give the answer they already know how to deliver, but they want to make sure you support the answer and you don't have an alternative way in mind. If you do, just tell them what that alternative is. By coming to you, they just want to be heard.

Sometimes, all it takes is a brief conversation like that to give the employee confidence since they'll feel you've got their back and understand their situation. But if you don't do that—if you pretend to be tough instead—you'll only make things worse for everyone.

What to Take Away from This

You may think of more than these six bad traits, but most likely, any others will turn out to be examples or manifestations of one of these six, probably the first, self-deceit.

The best leaders are self-reflective. They do not have oversized egos, and any pride they have is earned because their confidence matches their competence. They're good at what they do, they're confident in it, and now they have credibility because it all lines up. They're not idiots with huge egos.

Instead, they know why they do what they do.

4 | The Seven *Becauses* of Good Leaders

Terrible leaders try to be great ones, but good leaders just are. And they are good people because . . . yes.

Because. They have a *because,* a reason for going forward. Several, in fact. And this is where my work jettisons advice typically associated with integrity-based, purpose-driven leadership. Integrity, purpose, and the like are essential for goodness—leader or otherwise—but starting with *why*, as the saying goes, is not the best way to do that.

From *Why* to *Because*

Why is often the starting point, the question that propels us forward in our quest for meaning and success. It is the rationale behind our actions, the logical explanation for our choices. However, *why* can be akin to the first few notes of a symphony—necessary but not entirely revealing the depth of the composition.

Because, on the other hand, is the melody that flows through the entire piece. It is the deeper, more intrinsic driver of our actions. While *why* might point us in a certain direction, *because* is the force that keeps us moving, even when the path becomes challenging. It's the core belief, the unwavering conviction that resonates with our innermost values and passions.

To truly appreciate the power of *because*, we must first understand the limitations inherent in *why*. *Why* is often shaped by external factors—societal expectations, cultural norms, educational backgrounds, and even the influence of significant others in our lives.

It answers the question of motivation but doesn't always delve into the depths of purpose, which I will explain now.

Problems with Starting with *Why*

Yes, there are many. For instance, a *why* is:

Externally influenced. *Why* can be externally motivated. For instance, one might pursue a career in medicine because it's a respected profession in society (the *why*), but this may not align with one's inner passion or purpose (the *because*).

Changeable and uncertain. *Why* can change with circumstances. It might be dependent on specific situations or phases in life, making it a less stable foundation for sustained motivation and fulfillment.

The surface level of reasoning. *Why* often deals with the surface level of reasoning. It provides the immediate answer but doesn't always connect with the deeper emotional and psychological drivers that propel us forward.

Understanding the limitations of *why* opens the door to appreciating the richer, more resilient fabric of *because*. *Because* is not just an answer; it's a declaration of one's deeper self. It's the underlying narrative that shapes our life stories, the unwavering essence that endures through life's ebbs and flows.

The Power of *Because*

The journey to the heart of *because* reveals a realm where motivations are not just understood but deeply felt. *Because* is the soulful echo of our innermost desires and convictions, resonating with the core of who we truly are.

And we can take this further, from knowing about the power of *because* to actually applying it—and for us, that means writing *because* statements.

Most mission, vision, and other such statements fail to resonate with employees and customers because they are often abstract and disconnected from daily actions. A *because* statement, on the other hand, is deeply personal and connects directly to the core purpose of your business. It answers the fundamental question of why you do what you do, providing a powerful motivational force that drives your actions and decisions.

Brainstorming Your Because *Statements*

- **Reflect on your core motivations.** Consider what drives you at a fundamental level. Why did you start your business? What impact do you want to have?
- **Articulate your purpose.** Translate your reflections into a clear and compelling statement that captures the essence of your goal.
- **Live your *because* instead of bragging about it.** Good leaders who have to tell everyone they're good leaders . . .

are they really good leaders? No, that's an imbalance again, trying too hard to exercise soft power and thereby undermining your hard power.

Writing Your Seven Because *Statements*

But why seven? Because there are seven built-in motivations for every human being.

Have you ever heard of Abraham Maslow's hierarchy of needs? These five levels, seven needs in total, demonstrate what is essential for both surviving and thriving. The five levels are: Physiological, Safety, Love and Belonging, Self-Esteem, and Self-Actualization. For example, if your need for food and drink goes unfulfilled for too long, you're going to have a bad time. You won't worry about your self-esteem, for example, in that parched, starving state.

Each need builds on the previous one. Fulfill one, move up one layer or one need to fulfill, and so on and so forth until you reach the penultimate and ultimate needs to fulfill.

In the same way, there are levels of priority when it comes to good, purpose-driven, motivational (and motivated) leadership. These are the reasons for being good, for doing good. By understanding the hierarchy of needs, it becomes much easier to reshape any potential *because* statements you may have generated already and write all seven.

The safety and security level and the love and belonging level have needs that are similar yet different enough that we will count them separately: hence, seven statements instead of five. Here are some templates and samples for you. And the reason to do this exercise is to fully internalize leadership not as a job you do but as the person you are.

You must be a good leader not out of fear of losing the job, getting demoted, or embarrassing yourself. Rather, you must be a good leader because you cannot be anything but what you are. And *because* is the powerful linguistic vehicle for turning a desire to be a good leader into the reality of being that good leader. That should make sense. Especially when you recognize that the seven *because* statements are written as affirmations, not wishes. This is the way things are going to be, not how we hope they'll be. This is your new reality, new identity. So let's go.

Your Physiological Because Statement

I am a good leader because _____.
I am a good leader because I take good care of my people so they can take good care of theirs.

Your Safety Because Statement

I am a good leader because _____.
I am a good leader because I provide good, safe boundaries to protect my people from threats, both internal and external.

Your Security Because Statement

I am a good leader because _____.
I am a good leader because I am quick to praise and reward my people for doing the right thing.

Your Love Because Statement

I am a good leader because _____.
I am a good leader because I do what I believe is best for my people.

Your Belonging Because Statement

I am a good leader because _____.
I am a good leader because I place the right people in the right roles.

Your Self-esteem Because Statement

I am a good leader because _____.
I am a good leader because I believe in my people.

Your Self-actualization Because Statement

I am a good leader because _____.
I am a good leader because I show my people how to become good leaders too.

A Living Because

We are not living in the land of theory. All seven statements have been embodied in a real leader, a CFO named Carlton Merritt.

Physiological: Getting Better Benefits

One of the things Merritt understood at once was that he needed to give better benefits. To be competitive, the benefits he sought to give were peace of mind and showing that he cared about his employees.

While this sounds simple, it was a big deal for the team. It wasn't like he offered zero benefits, but he knew he could do better, so he offered mental health services.

Safety and Security: Providing a Haven

He also provided a safe place to discuss mental health with people who weren't employees of the company. He brought in a nutritionist, not to cater meals but to talk about healthy eating habits. He made the snacks a bit healthier as well. Though Merritt didn't have to do any of this, he cared enough about his employees' well-being to do it anyway. By doing so, he fostered genuine connections.

Love: Being in the Community

Like any good leader, he was in the community. A good leader doesn't lead only inside the four walls of the office but outside them as well. He created softball leagues and basketball leagues so people could not only have things to do but also feel as if they belonged.

Belonging: Praising Good Work

But there was another way he helped people belong—he had biweekly peer-review meetings. The leaders of his team would bring their direct reports and meet with him. Instead of doing the usual thing—telling them three things they did well and two things they did wrong—he emphasized all the stuff they did well, building the employees' confidence. Now, he did point out where they needed to improve, but he also had them take on more responsibility in areas they were strong at. By making a big deal out of his employees, he established a strong sense of belonging in them.

Self-esteem: Real Results Bring It

Everyone in the department was now hitting their goals, but more needed to be done. He wanted some more margin for error so there weren't any slowdowns. He went and asked employees what aspects of their job they hated because he figured that if an employee hated a certain aspect of their job, they would procrastinate on it, or they'd do it first but take a long time on it since they hated that part of their job. He made it clear that there was no judgment.

He also asked what they loved doing because if they could do that all day, they would be amazing at their jobs. His asking about all this served a vital purpose: it showed that saying you didn't like something didn't mean your job was on the line. Instead, he wanted to make sure employees loved what they were doing so they did more of it and, thus, helped out the company.

I asked Merritt why he was average. Why was he not exceeding expectations? It turned out that Merritt himself thought that hitting his goals was the thing to do. But I told him no, that wasn't enough.

Bill is the perfect illustration of this.

Why was Bill also handling customer onboarding? Shouldn't there have been someone from a different team handling such a thing? Having to close ten calls a day and onboard five new customers overburdened him since he had to put on his onboarding hat after he was done with his sales hat. He only had so much time.

But if Bill didn't have to worry about onboarding people, it was a big weight off his shoulders. And that's what happened. Because we had Bill handle only the closing of deals, his close rate went higher, to almost 60 percent, creating revenue for the company.

Having people specialize in what they love to do means fewer problems, fewer complaints, fewer service tickets. And now Bill and everyone else is exceeding their goals. Creating real results raised everyone's morale because now, no one falls short.

Self-actualization: Believing in Oneself

Merritt had to do a software migration, a process known to have a lot of pitfalls. He put in a newly promoted manager to head this project. Things went smoothly until day five of the migration, when there was a problem with the vendor. However, this new manager feared for her job because she ran into a problem that would make the process go from forty-five to sixty-five days. A delay like this was unacceptable.

But Merritt didn't treat it that way.

Instead, he said to her that these things happened from time to time. Her response would be what defined her, and he believed in her; otherwise, he wouldn't have put her there. All she had to do was hold her head up, take back control, and make sure that she delivered. If it would take sixty-five days, she should let the vendor know and make sure she delivered by that date because the problem was on their side anyway. The employee was stuck on the original forty-five-day timetable, worrying about all the costs that would come with a delay.

But Merritt made it clear that none of that mattered—the employee's responsibility was to keep pushing and see the job through to the finish line. This gave the employee the self-confidence necessary to go forward.

Being Who You Are in Real Life

There's another case of this with Darren. As a former military guy, he did not have much emotional intelligence—he was the "Get it done because I say so" guy. Darren's people believed in him, but he got an even better response out of them when he promoted from within. For example, he took one of his account managers and promoted them to agency manager. He gave people free rein to do things, but he also coached and supported them.

Take an employee of his named Mary. Before, he would have made her manager and told her to go do what she had to do. But now, because Darren has more emotional intelligence, Mary believes in him and doesn't want to let him down, so she became a leader he didn't even envision.

He couldn't have foreseen Mary's leadership before because, at the time, he had no emotional intelligence. But when he showed he had an open-door policy and he cared, things turned around. He allowed adults to be adults—and adults are leaders in their households. Just because they report to you at work doesn't mean they don't make decisions at home. Darren gave Mary many small projects, and those projects allowed her to build up her self-confidence and improve how she worked.

Putting Mary in situations that allowed her to win made all the difference. For example, when a new process for handling inbound calls was needed, she worked with the receptionist to figure something out. Similarly, when the renewal process was suffering, Darren asked Mary what should be done about it.

Darren's trick is presenting the problem, then asking someone what to do to solve it. He asks his employees how they would handle a given problem, then tells them to go do it. He did this with Mary, and the company was able to retain more customers. He brought Mary into hiring and onboarding new staff, to the point where Mary handles it all now. With all those things off Darren's plate, she is now the face of the business. So when a customer calls in, they don't need Darren. They go to Mary because Mary is now equipped to do that job. As before, real results led to self-actualization.

Be Who You Are
In both cases—Darren and Merritt—they followed all the *because*s since it was who they were, not who they were trying to be.

Repeat, affirm, and internalize these seven *because* statements, or use the templates to write your own, and you will become them. You will be a good leader.

But knowing your "because" is only part of the equation. To truly unlock your potential as a leader, you must identify and harness your unique strengths—those core qualities that set you apart and empower you to lead with authenticity, initially, and, eventually, with impact as well.

5

Identifying Your Core Leadership Strengths

Leadership is not a one-size-fits-all endeavor; it is as unique as the individuals who lead. That said, you may have heard the expression that history does not repeat but it rhymes. Good leadership is like that. There are essential skills to leading well, which we'll cover in subsequent chapters. But leadership is inclusive of all that you, the leader or would-be leader, are. You don't have to stop being yourself. In fact, we want you to be *more* of who you are.

Great-yet-not-so-good leaders have an air of inauthenticity about them, as if they are trying to portray that perfect Hollywoodesque image of the type of leader they are—a manager, a vice president, or even a "big shot" with great power *and* great responsibility. There's no need for that. What there is need for, however, is a mirror.

I wrote earlier that those most business-savvy struggle with leadership because they are so capable at doing the things they are supposed to be, as leaders, supervising others in doing. The book *The E-Myth Revisited* by Michael Gerber spends a couple hundred pages acknowledging this trap. When a specialist, technician, or otherwise worker bee starts a company—and therefore becomes its leader—they struggle to integrate their technical skill and natural aptitude into that leadership role. It's awful, actually. They "work *in* the business, not *on* the business." And the result is the company is headless. There is a leader who isn't leading; they're doing all the things that are *not* leading that they should be hiring and training others to do.

Expect this to be a temptation as you grow into a leadership role. Leading is unnatural when you haven't done it before—and when you've not seen good examples up close. This is likely the case for you, reading this now. So the purpose of this chapter is to help you **integrate** what you already excel at with your eventual (or imminent) leadership role.

How to Integrate Non-leader Skills into a Leadership Role

OK, I write that heading with a little bit of tongue in my cheek. We don't consider, say programming languages, a "non-leader" skill, technically speaking. But you get the idea, don't you? You're not coding in C# when you're running a meeting; running a meeting requires *separate* leaderly ability from programming prowess. It might just be a meeting of programmers, but there *must* be a guide for that meeting. This is the distinction for us to make. So, how do you "work *on* your people as a leader, not just *as* one of those people," to paraphrase Michael Gerber for our purposes?

I've identified eight key steps. Let's begin.

Eight Ways to Stay Great at What You Do While Leading It

The urge to jump in and correct your direct reports when they're doing the very thing you have done (or could learn to do) is going to be strong. But you won't have to. Here's what you can do instead—and yes, there's plenty to do.

Embrace Your Expertise

Your technical proficiency is your leadership's backbone (with one exception, which we'll cover in a later section in this chapter). To remain credible to your people and effective as one of them should you need to "hop back into that role" for any reason, you must stay on top of your game. Let's learn with some examples, not just with this first way but with the remaining seven.

- **For example,** if you're a software engineer turned manager, don't simply "manage" projects, asking for the usual reports. Actually join in coding sprints occasionally, even if it's just for the first hour, first day (or half of it), etc. This keeps your skills sharp and shows your team you're one of them. And it will help your self-confidence to prove to yourself that you've "still got it."
- **As another example,** consider a graphic designer who has moved into creative direction but decides to work very closely with certain high-profile clients. They could offer "VIP-level" service to the client, ensuring their design eye remains current, which benefits the designer, but also improves the customer experience for the client. *Wow, I'm special to this vendor,* is the intended thought.
- **And for our final example here,** let's imagine you're a scientist leading a lab. You might continue to perform experiments or at least review data with a critical eye to maintain scientific rigor. Better yet, where you have the

time, you might even attempt to duplicate (or see if that's possible) work or results that one of your employees or direct reports did.

Staying technically proficient means you understand the trenches where the real work happens. This matters to you, the one calling the shots, and also those below you on the organizational chart who are actually taking them.

Delegate with Care

Delegation is a necessity. So much so that Michael Gerber's book has spawned near-innumerable spinoff works covering management and reporting skills for professions like accountants, consultants, lawyers, and even dentists and landscapers. If you're going to make it as a leader, you've got to *lead*, which means you *must not do everything yourself*. Just think about it; what else will there be for your workers to do if you're doing everything, or trying to do everything you did *before* becoming a leader *and* fitting into your new role? You'll burn out. Many leaders work more than forty hours per week (closer to eighty to ninety in some industries), and you likely do not have the scheduling capacity (or energy levels) to work two jobs at once. What to do? Here are three quick examples that in some way, shape, or form apply to your industry and line of work as well.

- **For example,** if you're a chef who's now running a restaurant, delegate the daily menu preparation to your sous-chef but keep the unique or signature dishes under your purview.
- **As another example,** in a tech startup, you might delegate coding to your developers but retain oversight on the architecture of new features to ensure they align with your vision. This way you don't just get the final say in theory but in practice, and you'll know what exactly you are approving or requesting changes to in detail. The more you know!

- **And as a third example,** consider a marketing director who might delegate social media management to specialists or interns but attend their working meetings to offer feedback on ideas and even offer suggestions. The temptation will be to get too critical or too involved, however, so best to keep the intent to stay more of a watchful observer than command-and-control freak.

Ultimately, you get to choose what to delegate by assessing who can handle it and who needs to grow into it, which will empower your team without affecting output quality.

Manage Your Time Like a Leader

I brought this up earlier. It bears its own dedicated section for obvious reasons. Leadership demands different time allocations than individual contributions. Let's look at some examples once again.

- **For example,** a developer who becomes a team lead could schedule specific times during the week for hands-on coding, ensuring they don't lose touch with development while also dedicating time for team meetings and strategy sessions.
- **For example,** an architect now leading a firm might reserve mornings for design work and afternoons for client meetings, staff-management, and business development.
- **As another example,** a teacher moving into school administration might carve out time in their week to still teach a class or two, keeping them connected with the educational process.

Prioritizing leadership tasks means understanding when to lead from the front and when to step back into your expert role. As in all things, there is balance. At least, there should be!

Share Like a Mentor

The best way to shore up your knowledge base covering a given subject is to teach it to others. This is because thoughts are vibes but the uttered word crystallizes. This is why songs have music and lyrics. It's the feeling and the facts, the mood and the narrative. If we just "work" but don't "lead" that work, it's like we're playing classical music. This requires immense technical ability, of course, so don't get me wrong. But what is the story? Who's it about? I hear vibrant strings, drumbeats of great resonance, but . . . I don't have enough information to tell my friend who didn't attend the philharmonic orchestra what the symphony was about.

And so it is with teaching. When it's our turn to tell others what to do and how to do it—based on what we know and what we've done—we actually clarify our own understanding of it by doing the same for others. This, by the way, is why the most memorable and emotionally compelling public speakers have written bestselling books—they've already told that story in print, and it rocked readers' worlds. All that to say, you don't need to be afraid of teaching others what you do, because that is how you will also teach yourself more than you thought you knew. The student will become the master, but the master will become their own student . . . thereby achieving a new level of mastery. It's cyclical and reciprocal. That's pretty cool.

Here are three quick examples of this.

- **For example,** let's say you're a seasoned programmer. Perhaps you could hold regular coding workshops focusing on best practices you've learned over the years, fostering a culture of learning. You bring news on a new project you've heard about and what you would do if you were in your reports' role for recreating or otherwise repurposing that brilliance into the work here at this company.

- **For example,** a nurse manager might set up mentorship programs where they share critical care techniques or patient interaction strategies. Lunch-and-learns work best so busy nurses don't have to add yet another thing to a hectic day. They can do what they were going to do anyway, while receiving your mentorship. They can "digest" while they digest!
- **For example,** an experienced sales director could mentor their team through role-playing sessions on handling difficult negotiations or client pitches. These little sessions could also include appropriate self-deprecation to help sales associates feel comfortable. "You know, what you said there was good, but when I had this job, you know what I did? You won't believe it." And then that little anecdote of long-ago embarrassment can parlay itself into improvement the associate can make for their next real-world sales call.

By being a teacher, you reinforce your knowledge, grow your team, and ensure your expertise becomes part of the organization's culture. The way *you* do things can become the way *we* do things.

Continuously Learn

The world doesn't stop evolving, and neither should you. We've all heard stories of a patient coming in to see their doctor about an ailment, and the physician pulls out a tablet computer to begin googling around. This does not instill confidence in the consumer. We can all do better. Here's how.

- **For example,** a tech leader might take online courses on emerging technologies like AI or blockchain to ensure they stay involved with what's coming down the pike. They might also be able to "see around the corner" and guide the team or the organization away from pending industry doom that others didn't see coming because they weren't keeping up-to-date.

- **For example,** in the medical field, a department head could attend conferences to stay abreast of new surgical techniques or medical research. Just bring direct reports along, keep lots of notes, and send out a summary to the entire team afterward with the top five to ten learnings!
- **For example,** an executive in finance might pursue certifications in new financial regulations or study technologies like fintech. The edX.org website offers thousands of programs—from free online courses to full degrees—from the world's largest companies like Google and Amazon and Ivy League universities like Harvard.

Staying engaged in learning keeps you relevant and ahead—or at least at the same pace of your most curious employees. Know what's important before it becomes important, and you will become a highly-paid CEO. I virtually guarantee it.

Balance Hands-on with Oversight

I've touched on this before, but as with time management, there is a balance that cannot go understated. Finding the right involvement level is key to maintaining technical competence while avoiding the *E-Myth* that you can do it all even while leading it all.

- **For example,** a software company CTO might code a critical algorithm themselves but delegate the bulk of the coding to their team, focusing on architecture and direction. That's perfectly OK. Just make sure to screen-record all work so it can be turned into a tutorial for future efforts!

- **For example,** a construction project manager with a background in engineering might oversee the design phase but trust their team with the day-to-day construction. Just because you've been on-site on every job in the past lifting, hauling, pushing, moving, pulling . . . doesn't mean you need to be standing there watching other people do it every hour of labor.
- **For example,** a news website editor could draft headlines for major stories but leave the detailed reporting to their journalists, ensuring the narrative aligns with editorial standards.

In my experience, the sweet spot is where your hands-on contribution adds significant value, not where it micromanages. That is *no bueno*.

Innovate Through Your Expertise

The best leaders push boundaries—not just their own team's, but the industry's. If something has always been done one way, why not do it another? If there's a persistent problem that has a single accepted set of solutions, what would happen if you tried to do the exact opposite? Use your deep knowledge to push boundaries. It's fun; trust me.

- **For example,** a product designer turned leader might spearhead a new design methodology that leverages 3D printing for prototyping, setting their company ahead of competitors that use 3D sketches on paper. Believe it or not, that still describes numerous industries we all rely on every single day!
- **For another example,** consider a former researcher in pharmaceuticals who might lead the charge into personalized medicine, using their expertise to guide R&D strategies that are focused on precision care for every individual

patient. This is a hot topic in medicine right now, but more people are talking about it than doing it. Good leaders are both "hearers and doers," as the Bible says.

- **For example,** a tech company founder with coding skills might develop a new app feature that sets a standard in the industry, directly contributing to the product's evolution. Perhaps the platform and ones like it are always, only, or usually accessible via a web browser. What about the first (or first *good*) mobile app?

By driving innovation, you ensure your technical skills are not just maintained but are actively shaping the future. As a leader, your crystal ball can be your brain.

Self-reflect and Request Feedback

Leadership is a journey of continuous improvement. Sometimes it's painful. Every time it's necessary. I'll explain with some examples.

- **For instance,** a marketing executive might conduct quarterly self-reviews, asking if they're still producing creative content or if they've become too removed from the creative process. I actually got this idea from popular parenting books, which advise the counter-intuitive conversation parents can ask their kids—how have I been doing? It might be a little shock at first, but it will be worth it. Listen without interruption. Then you'll be the one shocked by what you learn.
- **For another example,** a software team lead could set up a feedback system where team members can anonymously suggest how the leader can better integrate their coding skills into management. This can actually be a way for that lead to work *in* the business, but in a way that their people want them to. Talk about the best of both worlds!

- **And as the final example,** a copywriting agency owner might check in with each of their writers to review various marketing and advertising campaign results. These reviews are always useful, but what's different this time is the onus of success is on the boss, not the contractor or employee. The owner, reviewing results, can ask their writers what *they* might have improved going into the project to uncover ways to increase client results that did *not* depend on the writer—but on the owner. This takes immense humility, as the owner is tempted to think, *You're the writer; it's your job to write words that sell.* But finding ways the owner could have helped their writers *better* find *better* words to sell *better* . . . that's as valuable to future campaigns as it is painful in the present moment.

You see, regular check-ins with yourself and your team help ensure you're not just leading but also excelling in your area of expertise.

And by following these steps, you will be able to maintain your technical edge while effectively leading your team. You will grow. Your people will grow. As they grow, so will you, and vice-versa. And your development as a leader will *not* come at the expense of what made you valuable in the first place.

Ten Troubleshooting Tips: When You Have No Experience in What You're Leading

I would be remiss to leave this out! This is the opposite situation we've covered so far in this chapter. It's like the flip side of the coin. There will be times when you have people reporting to you who have done the exact same work you yourself have done, yes. But at other times, you will be "the boss" over workers *doing things you have never done before and probably don't know how to do*. Here's how to handle that with ease and poise.

Acknowledge Your Lack of Expertise

I want you to be honest. It's OK to be transparent about your lack of direct experience in the area. For example, if you're leading a team of engineers but your background is in marketing, explain this to your team. "I know how to sell what you build." Honesty builds trust. "I'm new to the technical aspects of engineering, but I'm here to support your expertise and to learn from you."

Leverage Your Leadership Strengths

Consider non-obvious transferable skills. Even if you don't know the technicalities, you can bring qualities like strategic thinking and problem-solving to the table. For example, your (albeit relatively new) experience in managing projects or people can translate into understanding team dynamics and project timelines.

Learn Quickly

Immerse yourself in what you don't (yet) know. Actively seek to learn about the field you're leading. This could mean attending workshops or training sessions relevant to your team's work or reading up on industry trends or asking your team for reading materials or resources. Go to the Simple English Wikipedia page associated with your chosen subject matter. There you'll find easy-to-grasp explanations in easy-to-grok lingo.

Build a Knowledge Base at Work

Implement regular learning sessions where team members share knowledge. For example, you could start "Tech Talks" where engineers explain their work in layperson's terms to help you grasp concepts while fostering team collaboration. Just pipe up during the Q&A!

Empower Your Team

Delegate responsibly, as I wrote about in the previous section. Leverage your team's expertise by telling them what has to be accomplished and by when, *then get the heck out of their way*. For example, let your senior developer lead the technical strategy for a project, with you focusing on resource allocation and project scope. You don't have to do everything, which means you don't have to *decide* everything either.

Ask the Right Questions

Curiosity is leadership. It really is. When you show genuine interest in understanding someone's work, you make them feel like they matter, which, in turn, makes them feel like *you* matter. Curiosity is leadership. So, ask insightful questions that show you're engaged in learning from them. For example, instead of asking how something is done, ask *why* it's done that way or what alternatives exist, which can lead to innovation or better practices. It's possible they don't know! And look at you, already running a process improvement effort without technical expertise.

Trust and Verify

Balance autonomy with oversight. Trust your team's expertise, yes, of course, but it's wise to also establish checkpoints where you can review progress or outcomes. For example, set up regular review meetings where you can ask for explanations of processes or decisions, ensuring you're in the loop without micromanaging. Make it weekly or monthly, but not spaced further apart than that. Consistent check-ins that people know are coming help keep everyone on the same page.

Use Your Outsider Perspective

Remember, you have fresh eyes. Use them. Your lack of experience can be an advantage. You might see things from a different angle that insiders might overlook. For example, you might suggest a marketing approach to a technical problem that could open new avenues for problem-solving or product development. Beginner's luck means you might have a question that your team never knew even needed to be asked, but it's the one that changes everything.

Seek Mentorship Within Your Team

Reverse mentorship. Seriously. You can just do this. Encourage team members to mentor *you*. This not only helps you learn but also empowers your team, showing you value their expertise. Valued people value you back. So for example, you might pair with a lead technician for a couple of hours a week to learn the ropes of the machinery or software they use daily.

Network Outside Your Team

Expand your resources. Connect with experts in the field outside your immediate team for advice and learning opportunities. For example, joining industry groups or forums where you can learn from peers and experts in the field can be invaluable.

Leading without experience in the area you're managing requires humility, a willingness to learn, and strategic use of your existing leadership skills. Remember, leadership is not about knowing everything; nobody does. But, good leaders *do* know how to foster an environment where everyone can contribute to their highest potential.

Your core strengths are a vital component of personal and professional success even when you technically no longer "need" them. You know that saying "what got you here won't get you there"? That remains true, but what got you here, *you can bring with you*. It won't get you "there"—it won't make you the good leader you can be—but boy, it will help! You'll perform at your best, solve problems effectively, and contribute meaningfully to your team and organization even as you *lead* the things you used to *do*.

This is just the beginning of manifesting outwardly your inward leadership potential. The next challenge is ensuring others see and "feel" your leadership. So now it's time to learn how to use your voice and words to motivate, align, and lead with power, precision, and purpose. Let's go!

6

How to Speak (and Write) Like a Leader

Leaders lead. They don't ask for permission. They don't try to convince. They don't seek validation or approval. They don't cajole or patronize. They just know, and they just do. They operate with complete confidence and a calm, cool, and kind attitude in the public eye at all times. This is what good leaders do, and they do it by the way they talk.

Good Leaders Talk Like *This*, Not *That*

Communicate with Assuredness, Not Uncertainty

Perhaps. Maybe. Possibly. Might Be. Purge words of uncertainty from your speech because that uncertainty shows a lack of commitment. To present yourself as a leader, you must speak with assuredness. What you say is fact, even if it is just your opinion. You are the leader, so your word goes.

I Think. I Feel. Maybe. Saying these words is not a wise move. They relinquish your soft power and even cause people to doubt your hard power. You'll seem like an incapable leader, so an underling who feels they can do a better job will work to undermine you.

Leaders don't ask for permission. Asking for permission implies powerlessness; who are you seeking validation from? The one who has real power over you? No—you're the power. You're the decision-maker.

Likewise, don't try and cajole anyone. You don't need to talk anyone into following you; you know what action to take and take that action in the public eye at all times. Good leaders talk like they're in charge; they don't beg for permission.

Hold Frame; Don't Reveal Undue Emotion. Professional athletics is rife with examples of embarrassing overreactions over a perceived bad referee call, an errant shot or mistake midgame, utter despair upon loss, and the like. This is not good. I'm not going to try to tell sports superstars how they should act, of course; rather, let's acknowledge that these high-profile sports heroes set a very poor example of what leadership looks like, especially since many team captains often act the worst in public.

Who you are in public is who you are in private. For years, we watched as Tiger Woods lost composure over a sliced drive or missed putt. How you do all things is how you do small things. Who you are when everyone is watching is who you are when no one is watching. So it was no surprise when we learned that Woods, to put it lightly, acted without self-restraint in his marriage (and then lost his marriage, among other things).

In other words, who you are in public is who you are in private.

There is a time and place for emotion, even negative emotion, and that is in private. *Not* in front of your peers, your team, or anyone else who looks up to you.

Be Easy to Understand, Unlike a Textbook. Good leaders get their ideas across quickly and simply. They use short sentences. They do not wax and wane with literary eloquence and academic sophistication like they're PhD candidates, much like this sentence has been doing. No—keep it short, sweet, simple. An easy-to-read command is easy to follow.

Regardless of education, most people think, communicate, and comprehend on an eighth-grade level. When I learned that fact, it blew my mind, and it changed the way I communicated. Keep this in mind when you communicate in your own business.

Numerous emails and text messages have been leaked over the years from luminaries in the highest reaches of corporate America—figures like Steve Jobs, Elon Musk, and Jeff Bezos, among others. But what's always striking is how short and simple their writing tends to be. Musk, for example, can handle dense topics with two or three sentences, and those below him know what to do. It's not how many people expect them to write. They write with clarity and precision.

Think Concrete, Not Abstract. A key part of this clarity and precision is no analogies. Leaders who try to be great but fail tend to compare two things that aren't alike. They use analogies to explain themselves instead of comparing things directly; this is abstract, and confuses everyone.

Imagine I want you to send an important email to one of our company's top clients before the end of business today, but I explained the message's urgency by comparing it to the urgency of the protagonists in the Harry Potter saga to defeat the chief antagonist, Lord Voldemort. What does all that fluff have to do with the client? Are we saying our best customer is an evil wizard? We've left the real world and are now comparing a real situation to a fantasy novel, hoping the reader connects the dots. While it makes the writer feel clever, it doesn't help the reader.

Instead, just say what you mean. Hold frame.

Speak Low and Slow to Be High and Mighty. Easily fazed leaders know they're easily fazed, so they do their best to hide their lack of confidence. Their fear is easy to detect and gives them away. How so?

High-pitched uptalk and rapid-fire sentences.

It's as if they worry that they'll be cut off by the real boss, so they have to get it all out as quickly as possible. The faster the speech, the higher the voice. Statements incorrectly end with question marks or what sound like them.

Let's say you tell your team to meet back up at 1:00 p.m. for an important meeting, but you don't say it with any conviction. "Let's all meet back here at 1:00 p.m." comes off like "Let's all meet back here at 1:00 p.m.?" It sounds like a question, like you need approval. You're treating your workplace like a democracy when it's not. It's a place under your command—be it a team, a department, or the company as a whole. You are a benevolent dictator, the chief, the boss, the caudillo (to use the Spanish). The buck stops with you.

The judges of ancient Israel were appointed by God and thus whatever they said went. Their command was unquestioned, their rule absolute. Lest you think this an analogy, you are mistaken; you are not *like* a Spanish caudillo or a biblical judge of Israel—that's what you are, so act like it. It's OK to speak slowly in a lowered voice because your people hang on to your every word, and they are tuned in 100 percent, so there's no rush. Your speech is like currency—the fewer words you use, the greater the value of each of them. They're like gold; that's how good leaders talk.

But now, let's go to how bad leaders talk.

Reorganizing the C-suite

One of my clients hired me to reorganize their whole C-suite, and I jumped right into it. I interviewed the exiting party and helped hire the new party. It was an IT software company, once the star of the industry. And now their board needed a new CEO and a new COO.

The company was rife with missed deadlines and low morale. There was no certainty about the strategic direction of the company and its future plans. Because the board's income relied on the company doing well, they cared about this.

They flew to New York, then spent two weeks talking to the chairman of the board and two directors at large about what the challenges were. Then they met with the CEO and COO of the company. But because I was present, they knew the writing was on the wall.

But to hear the CEO and COO tell it, nothing was their fault. They blamed the board and whomever else they could. Then I told the chairman of the board he was right—we needed better leadership, or nothing else would change. I confirmed the condition of the company, then the company brought on a new CEO, whom we'll call Emma here.

Emma felt the weight of what she was entrusted with, but she rose to the occasion. When it came time to implement a new software system that would streamline our productivity, the IT team made sure they communicated with everyone regarding how it was going. Compared to the previous communication, Emma's communication was assured. She wasn't thinking about bringing a new software platform online; she got it done. She wasn't hoping it would deliver the right results; she knew it would. Emma gave the team clear assurance about what they were doing and why, as well as what the next steps would be. It's like bullet points: you say what you need to say in a short, declarative way. It's all well and good to write your emails this way, but you have to speak this way too because it makes your communication sound more certain.

That said, the goal here isn't to be some over-the-top forceful cartoon character, nor is it to be this meek and agreeable person who tries not to hurt anyone's feelings. You also don't want to let your emotions rule you. The point here is to be a real person with a real mission.

I was there with Emma when she had her first meeting. She wanted me there, as did the chairman of the board, and my job was to echo her sentiments. Emma said that she recognized the challenges the team had, but she was confident in everyone's collective ability to overcome them all, so let's focus on our strengths and tackle the issues head-on.

Contrast this with how the previous CEO spoke: "Hey everybody, this situation's bad, and we are in dire straits. Everybody's gonna have to buckle up and go along for the ride with me." This was two weeks earlier, before the new CEO was hired. He thought he was rallying the troops, but in truth, he was making the situation worse by showing himself to be weak willed. Emma didn't bother with that. She just said, "Let's get it done."

The previous CEO betrayed his lack of certainty in another way: he bragged about all his tech qualifications as if trying to see if I would like him. He took this behavior further by using big words, and his team noted that this was a habit of his. They'd rather he just told them what he wanted from them. Meanwhile, Emma just stated the goals: "Our goal this quarter is to increase customer satisfaction by 15 percent." Things like that.

There was also a contrast in how the different CEOs explained their goals. While Emma said to increase customer satisfaction by 15 percent by improving the speed and quality of our responses, the previous CEO gave a vague textbook of five pages of written goals. Emma spoke concretely while the previous CEO spoke in abstract terms.

There's a habit of corporate leaders going online and looking up quotes about leadership. I had a CEO who often did this, and he memorized about fifteen such quotes, which gave him motivation. (He thought the team was motivated by the quotes, too.) These were all quotes he didn't come up with, and his team knew he didn't come up with them. It was really hard for them to follow him and believe in him.

So, in light of that, I told him to cut that stuff out. There's no point in being false or abstract. If your motivation is to hit deadlines, let your inspirational quote be about hitting deadlines. Don't put up some Albert Einstein or Abraham Lincoln quote that isn't relevant to the issue at hand; you're not clever.

Instead, be yourself and be direct. If you've been slow on customer requests, say you're going to turn customer requests around in twenty-four hours. Make your intentions clear and concrete; don't hide them behind quotes.

Leader Voice

Earlier, I said to talk low and slow, as that conveys authority. That's because you have to find your leader voice, and low and slow is the way to do it. You need not only to be heard but also to be felt.

You need to convey authority and calmness because you feel those things. You feel as if you deserve authority because you do deserve it. You don't need to yell because leaders don't need to yell. When you speak in a low tone, the slowness calms the listener. It doesn't matter whether you're speaking in a private meeting or publicly on stage—always tell yourself that you have the authority. This is a good solution for a leader who doesn't know how to do this already—low equals authority, and slow equals calm. Whether you're typing or speaking, that's what you want to hear.

And how do you type that way? Let's go back to something I mentioned earlier—bullets, not paragraphs.

Don't just type in bullets; speak in bullets. It keeps you from rushing because rushing shows nervousness. With bullets, you know you're in control. You know what your next points are.

But you also need to practice.

Rehearsal (Yes, You Need This)

Speaking with authority is a skill, and like all skills, you need to practice it. But how do you do that when it's not second nature—when you haven't been a public figure, when you haven't had media training, when you weren't on the university debate team, when you don't have an MBA or any other relevant experience?

You take the first step. You go and do it. That next email you respond to? You go and do it. That next presentation you have to give? Do it. For leaders, practice comes when you do. You don't go home and rehearse with your spouse or your children—it doesn't work that way because that's a fake environment. It has to be a real situation, right in front of you. You can't go to a supervisor and say, "Let's role-play for a minute." You have to put in actual action—that's your practice.

That said, if you're the leader, hire a coach to help you out. It's like a sports team—you know when the game is, so you practice all these scenarios with your coach. However, the real test of a leader is responding in the moment. Hire the coach, keep reading this book, memorize what you need to know, but make sure you get yourself into as many real situations as possible. And if you have questions, talk to the coach.

A Bias Toward Action

You have to break your own wheel a little bit.

This isn't an analogy either; it has something to do with what you're physically doing. In this case, it's speaking or writing because you're doing it with your body. Just as you practice a swing with a baseball coming at you; you cannot learn to bat by reading a book. You can't learn to be a persuasive leader by reading a book—not even this one. It can point you in the right direction, but it's something you have to practice. So go out there and do it. It's the only way to learn.

Communication builds connection, but a compelling vision creates direction. In the next chapter, you'll learn how to cast a vision that unites, motivates, and drives your team toward a shared goal.

7 | How to Cast a Vision People Will Follow

When I was ten years old, I heard Les Brown say, "You have greatness within you."

For me, hearing that was compelling because I had not only a great example of what a man should look like but also a vision of what a leader should look like, and I saw it at an early age. Seeing that told me something important: be the person you want to follow. The truth is your greatness expands beyond the words you say into the actions you do. That meant that if I was to be the person others followed, my actions mattered more than my words did.

So at ten years old, I started figuring out how to make my actions speak louder than my words.

To be the natural leader I wanted to be, whether in school or in my own business, I had to do what everyone else was willing to do, and because of that, I never had to bark orders. If something needed to be done, I led by example and showed the way. For me, vision was all about action.

But how do you define *vision*?

Vision

Martin Luther King Jr. had a "dream," but I had a *vision*. A vision is a clear plan in which you can see the steps on how to get there, whereas a dream is a vague wish. In a dream, your eyes are closed, but with a vision, your eyes must be open. You have to look at where you're going and what problem you want to solve. You have to be able to see it.

Now there are three visions that stand out in both history and recent times: the founding of America, Martin Luther King Jr.'s vision of a better society, and Elon Musk's popularization of electric vehicles.

The Founding of America

This was a vision like no other. Just like the Pilgrims came over to build their shining city on a hill, the American founders knew what they wanted, and it took leadership of all kinds to get there. Even though they sought to build a country that valued liberty, they couldn't have people aimlessly doing whatever—everyone needed a vision to guide them toward ultimate victory.

Martin Luther King Jr.'s Vision

While King said he had a dream, I think we just might be able to recast that dream as a *vision*. Less than a hundred years before this writing, African Americans didn't have equal rights. They were also denied the right to vote, and they had to attend segregated schools. King wanted a world where anyone could rise through excellence and merit, as opposed to their ancestry, and he articulated that vision before missions—and died for it.

Elon Musk's Vision for Electric Cars

Before Musk came along, electric cars were seen as a joke. To most people, they were some loony pipe dream that weren't practical for ordinary people. Twenty years before this writing, you'd get laughed at if you said you wanted an electric car.

But things have changed. Thanks in part to Musk's company Tesla Motors, electric cars are everywhere now. And because they're everywhere, infrastructure such as charging stations has been built to allow for recharging them on the go.

Musk worked on this concept silently, out of the media spotlight. It took vision to make this the new way people got around. With all this focused effort, electric vehicles went from a punchline to a mandate in the state of California by 2028. When something like that happens, you know you have changed society in a fundamental way.

The Problem a Vision Solves

The problem leaders always have is "What am I supposed to do?" The vision solves that problem because you can see, in a concrete way, what you have to accomplish and, thus, what you have to do. When you have your goal in front of you, the steps lay themselves out one at a time in an obvious way. There might be a lot of them, the path might be difficult, but you know what the steps are, and you can't miss them. You become immune to uncertainty and ignore all distractions.

What dooms every person with drive is "shiny-object syndrome." When you get involved in a long-term project, you've been looking at it for so long that it's no longer as dazzling to you as it was when you started. You're stuck in the middle, and it's dark and dingy. You don't want to be here anymore. But while you're amid the grime and grit of the work, you see something in the corner of your eye—a shiny object.

This shiny-object syndrome causes otherwise top performers to fail to live up to what they're capable of. Instead of working through the hardest part of a worthwhile and meaningful project, they chase whatever grabs their attention. But those things are mirages, leading them astray from what they should be doing. We all know people who chase mirages forever. They move from job to job while starting this or that side hustle. But they never accomplish much. They get a couple of customers, then all of a sudden, they switch to a different product or a different market. They have no clear plan, and they don't know why they're doing what they're doing.

In other words, there's no vision.

If you ask what their vision is, you often get a number—maybe they want to earn $10,000 per month, $1 million per year, or some other figure. That's the sum total of their vision, and it's terrible because there are no steps to get there. Wanting to earn some set amount of money isn't a vision; it's a want. It's not even a means to an end—it *is* the end. It doesn't help you because you don't know what you're supposed to do next. You could do anything and everything.

People who fall victim to shiny-object syndrome can experience a real mental health issue over chasing something that wastes years or even decades of their lives and doesn't get them anywhere. But to achieve what you want regarding your career or your personal finances, you must have a vision that leads you on the right path and helps you avoid the wrong path. You do only the things that get you closer to the vision and avoid everything that doesn't. You can only speak with confidence when you have a vision.

Having a vision helps you avoid anything that's a time suck. When doing something, ask yourself: "Will this help me get what I want more of?" If it doesn't but you feel excited about it, it's a shiny object and you should stay away from it.

But the real benefit of a vision comes from what it does for a team. Just as it protects you from uncertainty, it protects them too because everyone will know the goal and their role in making it happen. You don't want stressed workers asking why they're doing a given task, coming in an extra night or an extra week to get something done that's not in their job description. "Why are we working on this third-party project? Why is a consultant in here telling us what to do? Why are we using this new software?"

Questions like this create uncertainty, and uncertainty decreases the perception of authority. If your team doesn't know what they're doing, you don't know what you're doing either. And because of this, they become distractible by backstabbing, and they silo themselves in little cliques or plot mutiny against the boss. You don't want any of that to happen.

Without vision, the people perish.

Visioneering

It's all well and good to have a vision, but how do you get one? That's where visioneering comes in. Visioneering is when you have a vision, you communicate it, and you get it going. You start to make progress toward it instead of treating it as some airy wish.

The vision has to be driven by you. As leader, you must provide the momentum needed to make the vision a reality. Leaders go first.

What does a leader have? Followers. A leader doesn't have co-leaders because they don't exist. Anyone who tries it fails. Too many organizations have leaders who treat the team as co-leaders, not understanding that they have the hard power and need to use it. However, you also need the soft power so people follow you willingly, instead of dragging their feet and grumbling.

Visioneering begins with a vision, and that's seeing what's possible, what ought to be, and how you want things to be different. It's not enough to say what you don't like in this industry or this company; that's an anti-vision, not a vision. Anti-visions don't work because they're focused on the thing you don't want. In many ways, it's worse than the $10,000 goal because not only do you have no path, but you also have no goal. You don't want bad reviews, you don't want weak word of mouth, but you haven't said what you do want.

And vague goals like "have the highest customer service satisfaction ranking" don't work either because they're too abstract. But when your goal is "make contacting our company the best memory of a client's entire day," you have something you can grab onto because you can take steps toward it.

To accomplish that goal, you'll need to train your people to communicate with absolute empathy. You'll need to anticipate customer responses. You're going to give people the sales training and technical support they need to build rapport with angry customers. When customers call, they're in a bad space, so how do you turn that around? With your people trained, you know what you need to do, what solutions you need to implement, and how to test them so you know you're improving. It's so unheard of that it summons the best from people.

That's what good visions do—they make the average person say, "Is that even possible?" And they have a role in making that impossible thing real. It's possible when they fulfill their role along with everyone else.

And everything is so neatly laid out. You're doing some training. You bring in new software. You have a record of every customer, and you know customers hate being asked for their name and number when they're regulars. So using the software, everything pertaining to the customer is in one place; you know when their birthday is and how many kids they have. You know their personality quirks. You don't need to be any kind of specialized expert because all the information is in the software.

Be Positive About Your Vision

Having all this information on hand makes it easy to implement a vision in which calling your customer support line is the best memory of a customer's day. Because the experience is positive, they'll double their order instead of getting angry and demanding a refund. That said, you won't be able to do this every time.

Based on how vivid your vision is, you can put additional objectives in front of it. A powerful enough vision will make people wonder if it's even possible (in a good way). That's better than a negative vision about not sucking at customer service. Even if you're not on Apple's level when it comes to customer service, a vision of making customer service calls into great experiences will be unexpected. You can even send little gifts as thank-yous for calling.

This visioneering, making concepts real and concrete, is so much better than the way vision development is usually done: through writing exercises that make an idea look more like a job description. While there's nothing wrong with writing down one's vision, these job description–style notions are often abstract because you can't see the goal. What does it mean to be the best whatever anyway? A good way to see if your ideas make sense is to try and imagine it in your mind's eye. Not being bad at customer service isn't something you can imagine like that, but anyone can imagine the best moment in their day because they know what that means to themselves.

But above all else, the action needs to be written into it. Your vision will be the thing that's out of reach to you, a thing you can visualize. If you can see this out, you win everything. In fact, one trick you can do is to make your company the tangible opposite of what people don't like about companies such as yours. Add a *because* after the vision statement to make it stick—it will become so much more powerful as a result.

The simpler the better; you don't need paragraphs upon paragraphs. One thing I often do is throw out existing vision statements because they tend to be too wordy, and no one reads them anyway—not employees, not customers, no one. I once worked with a nonprofit that had a very long mission statement, and we simplified it down to say "Our vision is to end hunger and ensure food security for all because no one should have to go to bed hungry." Short and simple, with a strong *because* statement at the end—that's impact.

When I do exercises like this with my executive clients, it becomes really heartfelt, and their vision becomes much clearer. Instead of having a marketing company create it, the leader does so.

Les Brown's Impact

Les Brown's vision was the opposite of what I had observed and lived in my young life. The focus on action, the focus on tangible results—that made things real for me in a way that nothing else did. I've carried this forward in both my work and my life, and I'll make sure to help others in the same way that he helped me, even if he didn't realize it.

While a powerful vision inspires, team alignment ensures it is executed effectively. Next, we'll dive into practical ways to strengthen unity and collaboration within your team.

8

How to See the Best in People When They Give You Their Worst

Effective leadership is dealing with people who don't want to be followers.

One thing any leader must understand is that just because someone isn't a leader in the organization doesn't mean they aren't a leader at home or in their community. You have to give that person their due respect.

But even if you do everything right, there are people who don't want to get along, acting like problem children. Indeed, that might be more true than you realize; you may *feel* young, but compared to a nineteen- or twenty-year-old intern, you may as well be a geezer. Plus, that intern may be there for college credit, and you can't really fire them. Even if you did have the authority to fire them, you might not want to.

On the other hand, you can have a problem employee who's way older than you who believes they should've been appointed to your position. Thus there is immense envy, and they'll try to sabotage you.

In the face of this, you'll want to punish them, but you might want to be careful there.

The Pitfalls of Punishment

One thing you can do is punish the person or people causing all these problems—fight fire with fire, as the saying goes. But that doesn't work because they have the power to walk away. Where you exercise the soft power of being tough, they exercise the hard power of leaving, and if they were fulfilling crucial roles, you're stuck in a bad position. It can even look bad on your resume because you're not good at keeping employees around, and no one's going to investigate the full story of how that happened.

The point is that tit for tat won't end in your favor.

That said, leaving the issue alone won't help you either. That risks the problem people winning others to their side, spreading rumors about you, and weaving conspiracy theories. With the power of workforce manipulation, everyone will have turned against you. You can't fire everyone, and even if you did, they'd tell everyone that you were a chore to work for.

You may want to focus on where they're going wrong—after all, that's what happened when you were in school. The teacher made it a point to look at where your grades had slipped, then had you focus on those. Thus, one would assume the employee would appreciate being told where their problem areas were.

But one would be wrong.

Outside the educational environment, you do what you're best at. You don't get paid to build up your skills but to use them. Focusing on your employees' faults won't get you far; in fact, what you give attention to increases, so hammering on your employees' faults will just blow up in your face. If you want more negativity, focus on that. But if you want more positivity, focus on the positive, and see the good in your employees.

Indeed, there are better ways to handle problem employees.

A Better Route

Listen First

When you are talking to them, do not talk over them. Do not interrupt them, even if they sound like whiners. Before you respond, wait until they're done, and make sure you actually hear them instead of just waiting your turn to talk. Show that what they have to say is important. That alone may be an improvement over what they're used to. And the best thing to do is understand things from their perspective. Know what's going on in their world so you can feel what they feel. They may have been promised the job you now have, or they're an intern, and the job they're doing now has nothing to do with what they studied. They may feel their abilities are wasted, or they're being given tasks no one else wants to do. Because they feel they're being disrespected as people, they disrespect you back.

Instead of yet another lecture, do some visioneering. Talk to them about what they want from the company, and when you need to discipline them, have it be a positive thing. Talk about what harmony you see them creating inside the organization. Amplify the positive, and stop spotlighting the negative.

Lead with Empathy

A common complaint among older folks is that young people have gotten too soft. They claim that all the misbehavior, all the disorder, all the disrespect that young people supposedly show comes from the people in charge not being tough enough to beat these young punks into shape. So you decide you're not going to be some softy pushover; you're going to get tough, and you're going to make sure those disrespectful twerps learn their lesson. No more Mr. Nice Guy!

Yeah, stop that. Now.

Being a bargain-bin drill sergeant will not get you the respectful, obedient employees you want; it'll only get you employees who put on a show of respect while hating your guts and doing everything possible to undermine you. Instead, your task is to lead with empathy.

Far from showing weakness, leading with empathy allows you to understand what may be troubling those under you. Most of your employees aren't snakes trying to take advantage of you; they genuinely want to do a good job. Hear them out, and give them a chance to show what they can do. In most cases, they just want to be listened to. You'll find that the negative behavior they showed before will clear right up, and they'll be happy and productive afterward. Remember, you're running a workplace, not a prison or a boot camp; you want the employees to feel valued, not humiliated.

But what if they continue to misbehave? What if they are dishonest? Then, and only then, do you punish them. When you first talk to them, you explain in clear language what your expectations are. If they fail to meet those expectations, then you can let them know what they did wrong and take appropriate action. Even here, you don't shout at them. Just be firm, and don't let them draw you into their negative behavior. You are adults working for real money, not children fighting over a cookie.

Redirect Negativity

"An eye for an eye leaves the whole world blind." That quote, often attributed to Indian independence activist Mahatma Gandhi, is the stone-cold truth in many places of work.

Get the tit-for-tat thinking out of your head because employees will walk away if they feel they aren't being treated with dignity, regardless of the pay. In a negotiation, the party who can walk away has the upper hand, and you need the employees more than the employees need you. Going forward with your little tit-for-tat games will leave you short staffed, even if your employees have to endure a grueling job search.

Nobody wins in that scenario.

Instead, take their negativity and flip it. Don't focus on all the things they did wrong or all the areas you think they need to improve on; instead, focus on areas where they've done well, highlighting the places you think they're strong. Focusing on weaknesses may be good for skill building, but no one is hired for the things they're bad at, so focus on the things you hired them for instead. They'll feel much more respected because they'll feel their skills are being recognized, and that positivity will motivate them to do better and guide them toward their potential. You will have turned confrontation into transformation.

However, while it's good to talk about these things in the abstract, we need to see these principles in action, helping a real person solve real problems with disrespectful employees. Let's see how Kristi turned a potential disaster into a success story.

Kristi's Big Lesson

I had a client named Kristi who was new to her leadership role. She had been in the position for about a year, and she had a senior employee with an obvious chip on her shoulder. Kristi's initial reaction was to crack down and show her who was boss. She thought she was asserting her leadership, laying down the law.

But all she did was fuel the fire.

So when Kristi came to me, she was planning on terminating that employee. Thus, her reason for hiring me was to rebuild the workflows that would be disrupted by the bad employee's removal. But first, I wanted to talk to her about why she was firing that employee. She told me how she got the position and how this senior employee kept challenging her authority.

So I asked her the obvious question: Had she tried sitting down with the employee and listening?

She told me it wouldn't work. I asked why, and she said that the senior employee had a chip on her shoulder. So I instructed her to listen to this employee—not just to the words but to the underlying frustration as well. People don't just act out like that; there had to be something there.

What Kristi discovered was that the employee felt undervalued. She felt unheard, and she believed her ideas were being overlooked because she wasn't a manager or director. When Kristi came back to me with this information, I suggested trying a different approach.

Instead of terminating her, acknowledge her concerns. Give her a small project to lead. Give her something she can take ownership of. Most of the time, when adults feel they're in control of something important, there'll be an attitude shift toward more constructive behavior. If there isn't, then Kristi is right to fire this person. So I coached Kristi on how to have that conversation in which she saw the potential in her wayward employee.

After ninety days, not only was this small project completed, but this turned out to be one of Kristi's most productive employees. The employee's attitude changed for the better. Within six months, this person was a team leader. Today, Kristi has been promoted, and this once-bothersome employee is now the director of the marketing department. But it all started with listening to frustration, not going in with hard power and pounding someone into shape. She went out with a different idea: see if hearing the needs can turn into potential.

And turn it did.

It really was that simple. The employee felt like she had no voice, so Kristi figured out a way to give her a voice. Kristi started her small, but the employee owned it. The employee realized she had the autonomy to do something big for the department and the company as a whole. Kristi even helped her organize a team for the project, despite there being no team lead position.

And this new team rallied behind this employee who was deemed negative for going against the status quo and not giving the full effort. All that needed to happen was for the employee to feel seen, to feel heard. She needed not only to be allowed to give her opinion, but also to implement it to see what happened. But now, she has a team of about twenty and won a big marketing award within the company a couple of years ago, so the company recognized her efforts after she felt ignored for so long.

That's the mark of a good leader.

However, this is only the bare minimum for showing effective leadership. Once you've gotten your employees' respect, you need to go further. You need to learn a set of rules you cannot break if you want to keep your leadership position and, just as importantly, to keep the respect from your people that your position deserves.

9

The Ten Unbreakable Rules for Trustworthy Leadership

Let's talk about a guy named Ryan.

Ryan owned a business, but he was having some challenges from his team with deadlines. He would say, verbatim, "I need this ASAP." He would say that all the time, no matter what.

But one time, he got called to the mat for needing something ASAP.

He had asked his team to finalize a video package delivery. His marketing manager worked late; she put everything else on hold to get this done. After she submitted the finished product to Ryan, she was shocked that Ryan hadn't reviewed it yet. It turned out that Ryan hadn't planned on presenting the video for two weeks, but he had told everyone it needed to be done ASAP.

The manager was furious. She had pushed everything aside, assuming that the project needed to be done on short notice, and it just so happened that he didn't need it for the next two weeks. Had she known how much time he had, she could have not only given Ryan better quality, but she also could have gotten her other work done.

This made Ryan realize there was a clear lack of communication. He hadn't told his manager everything she needed to know, and now she felt like she'd been suckered. In fact, a lot of employees felt this way once this incident came to light. How much had Ryan been lying about deadlines? Maybe he didn't need things ASAP after all.

The manager told Ryan to his face that he had lied. The employees went through everything Ryan had said he needed ASAP, and it turned out that he hadn't needed them done so quickly. If the company had missed a deadline one time and needed a fast turnaround on everything else, Ryan should've been upfront about that. If he wanted to punish people for missing a deadline, he should've been upfront about that, too. But he shouldn't have lied to everyone and said everything was critically needed. In doing so, he crushed the team's morale and made things more difficult for everyone.

Which leads us to our first lesson.

Lesson #1: Don't Lie, Even by Omission

Your justifications don't matter. Your excuses don't matter. Your biases don't matter. Whatever you do, don't lie.

Lying makes you look like you can't be trusted, that the things you say have no meaning. You could be saying one thing but mean another. When you give orders, no one knows if the deadline you set is when it's due or even if your orders are the right ones. The confusion and mistrust that lying creates are not worth whatever short-term benefit you get from it.

This includes lies by omission as well. Hiding crucial information is just as bad as giving incorrect information because what you're hiding may be important to the person you're talking about. If you tell someone something but leave out important information, you've left them unprepared for unexpected complications. They'll go back to you and tell you what happened, only for you to admit you left some information out. That will break trust as surely as bad information would, so don't do that either.

All this means being upfront about expectations, timelines, and goals. When I explained this to Ryan after the video debacle, he didn't like hearing it at first. But, at the same time, he also understood that he had to set those goals upfront because if he didn't, he'd come off as someone who couldn't be trusted. One thing we did was remove ASAP from our vocabulary; we would not use that term anymore because it gave him too many chances to mislead people about timelines. We also implemented some project management software so everyone could see not only when the big projects were due but also when all the milestones within a given project were due. This way, there was full transparency—no more worries that Ryan was misleading anyone about when things were due.

Ryan learned his lesson when his employees called him out. Calling people out can be a powerful tactic when done correctly, but one thing you must never do is call someone out in public.

Lesson #2: Never Judge in Public

Chances are you've heard of the term "cancel culture." It's when a mob forms on social media to call out a target for real or perceived misdeeds, frightening and embarrassing the person. It doesn't matter whether the person committed an actual crime or merely said something that went against the cultural consensus; the fury is the same. Associates, friends, and even family distance themselves from the target, causing them to feel isolated; oftentimes, the target loses their job. The aim is to extract a humiliating public apology from the target, cementing their tormentors' control over them. There are no rules of evidence involved, no due process—just a towering tidal wave of emotion, destroying everything in its path.

Judging someone in public is a lot like canceling them—you put them on the spot and whip up negative emotions around them because no one wants to be next. Singling someone out for scorn and criticizing someone in front of their coworkers—I've seen a lot of this, and even people on my team have behaved this way.

I had to talk with one of my own team members about this. We were in a team meeting once with about fifteen to twenty people. We were going all around giving various updates, but then one employee called another one out because, while the first employee had done everything on time, the other employee had not. The first employee even said that they would lose a client if they didn't get ahead on their deliverables, a remark meant to shame the second employee even more. Even though we were pretty close knit as a team, calling someone out in public like that was uncalled for. Plus, it turned out that the employee had a valid reason for being behind on the work; that employee had even readjusted their ninety-day plan, though those notes were not visible to everyone. Nonetheless, this callout caused some animosity between the employees, and I, as team leader, had to fix it.

And fix it I did. Since the callout was public, my response was, too. I said that these things weren't what we did. We would handle things in private, but as a unit, we didn't talk about family in front of family. And if we didn't know the whole story, we didn't rush in without details or context.

Humiliated employees are resentful employees, and you do not want resentful employees because they'll do everything to sabotage you. Those employees will perceive you as a tyrant, and tyrants do not last long. But public callouts aren't the only way you can end up humiliating an employee. Stealing credit for something they've done is another way this can happen.

Lesson #3: Never Steal the Credit

Employees want to feel valued for what they do. They don't want to be seen as just a number pumping out product but as someone who brings value and helps the company prosper. They want to be proud of their work, putting to use the skills they honed in school. After all, those skills are why you hired your employees in the first place.

So when you steal the credit, you've disrespected them in a big way. You've turned a team effort into a one-person show, rendering everyone who made your success possible invisible.

I had a client named Chris (not Chris Paradiso), and he would always steal credit. If there was a team success or a team journey, Chris would go back to senior leadership and say that he had done a great job, and he couldn't wait to lead the next project or bring the next client on board. Any time a major project was completed, Chris would be the first to claim victory. His team, who worked weekends and late nights to get everything done, felt betrayed and unappreciated because he never highlighted their contributions. He would always hold the team accountable to make sure things got done, but he would never talk about them when it came time to explain the projects' success.

Chris came to me and asked why his team was so disengaged and resentful. I let him know that he was breaking the rules, that there's no *I* in *team*. To his credit, he took what I said seriously. He went to the team, apologized like an adult, and even went to senior leadership to apologize for sidelining the team so much. To make up for his earlier behavior, he gave all five of his team members a raise, just to let them know they were appreciated for everything they did. He didn't want to take credit for everything anymore. What he did made his team come together.

And after all this, Chris still benefited by eventually becoming COO of the company.

Stealing credit causes problems while giving people their due helps everyone, even you. On the other hand, you must also avoid another huge pitfall, the opposite of stealing credit—pinning blame.

Lesson #4: Never Blame

Much like calling out someone in public, pinning blame creates resentment. In this case, it doesn't matter whether you blame the person in public or in private—marking someone as "the reason everything has gone wrong" is a big mistake. Even if you think their actions led to bad results, keep that to yourself and accept the blame. Otherwise, the employee will feel resentful, and that's always bad news.

In my consulting company, we pride ourselves on being results oriented. However, we don't get results every single time, though most times we do. But as CEO of the company, when something doesn't go right, I always shoulder the responsibility. It is never a team member's fault. If things didn't go as expected, it's on me because either I wasn't clear, I didn't set the right expectations, or I didn't follow up or follow through.

A good leader never blames anyone because it makes them look like they're avoiding responsibility. As leader, the buck stops with you, so if there's an issue, it's your job to understand it, correct it, and prevent future occurrences of it. You never hand responsibility off to an underling and act like you played no part in the failure.

There is no one to blame but you, so don't pass the blame for any reason.

When you do blame someone, it comes across like you're attacking them to their core. You are making it seem as if their actions made the project collapse when they were just doing their best. You come across as accusing them of sabotage. Making them feel like a criminal when they could only do so much will turn the work environment toxic all by itself.

And you will get feedback from this—feedback you shouldn't resist.

Lesson #5: Never Resist Feedback

Feedback is essential information. You need it to make accurate decisions, even if the feedback is not what you want to hear because reality exists regardless of what you think. Surrounding yourself with sycophants who approve of your every move may make you feel good, but it won't lead to good decision-making.

What you want from the world, put out into the world. If you want people to accept your influence, you must accept theirs. Even if their ideas are terrible, they need to feel comfortable sharing those ideas with you.

And sometimes, those ideas lead to small wins.

Lesson #6: Never Overlook Small Wins

Every win matters, no matter how small. It's hard enough to get any kind of victory, so when you get a win, celebrate it.

Something happened after I sold my agency. Since I oversee a four-hundred-person team, I always think in terms of the big picture. One day, I had a manager come to me; his name was Cordero. He explained to me that not everyone has the intensity I have. I had them do a project in a ninety-day sprint, and they had gotten pretty far by day thirty and thus wanted to celebrate. But I was stubborn and said the job was for ninety days, and until we reached that ninety days, we hadn't won, and we shouldn't celebrate. Cordero disagreed, saying that everyone was working hard, and if we didn't celebrate, there would be ninety-day sprint after ninety-day sprint, and we wouldn't celebrate until the end of the year.

I put myself in the team members' shoes, and it turned out he was right. If I only celebrated at the end of the fourth ninety-day sprint, I was not showing them that they were appreciated. I was not showing them that I was proud of their work.

And so one of the biggest lessons I learned early on was just that—celebrating small wins. Even though it goes against the fabric of who I am, I celebrate, knowing that not everyone is like me. Thus I make it a practice to celebrate the small wins.

So I retooled things a bit. I pointed out the big goal, then pointed out all the milestones along the way. And at milestones, we celebrate. We pump our fists as a team because you never know who needs that boost. Leaders, especially driven type-A leaders, should know that not everyone wakes up super intense. If you don't celebrate the small wins, you're in jeopardy of this becoming unnatural. You want winning to become a habit, so reward those wins; that way, you'll get more of them.

And they'll see more of you, too.

Lesson #7: Never Isolate Yourself

You don't want to become aloof from your employees. They need to see you so your presence feels real, and they feel you're working alongside them instead of goofing off while they're doing all the hard work. Now, you may not see it this way—in fact, you're the opposite of a slacker. You're grinding earlier than everyone else, and you don't want to be bothered while you're doing all this. But there's power in being visible. There's credibility in being visible.

I'm the sort of person who's in there grinding from 7:30 a.m. until 7:30 p.m., but no one's seeing me do that, so it might as well not exist. Something I learned from Bill Astor is how important it is to be visible. He would call it doing a walkabout. The idea is to just walk outside and be visible to everyone. You need to have a smile on your face, and you need to go out and acknowledge people; it will always be appreciated.

On the other hand, when you isolate yourself, you're saying one of two things: either you're the most important person in the office, or you contribute little. If you don't need to talk to anyone, then you've got it all figured out. If you've got it all figured out, there's no need for a team. Conversely, if you've got it all figured out, you're not putting that knowledge to use. So even if you are, in fact, the most important person in the office, don't give off that vibe. Make people feel they're part of the team. Make people feel they're part of the decision-making.

We live in the age of the remote meeting, so a walkabout may not be possible. You can make up for this with a few five-minute meetings a day, just so everyone doesn't feel isolated from each other. It may feel like you're just being social, but it's actually a morale boost.

Be careful not to be too repetitive with it; you don't want people being able to predict when your walkabouts happen because then they won't take them seriously. That said, make a broad schedule for how you're going to do them; you don't have to explain it. And when you're out there, talk to your employees. When I do it, it saves me multiple team meetings. I do ten-minute check-ins with my COO, my VP of sales, my top sales rep, or even my mid-tier sales reps. You never know when someone just needs a morale boost from seeing you, the leader, caring about them or having a conversation with them.

And sometimes, those conversations can be difficult.

Lesson #8: Never Avoid Difficult Conversations

Sometimes, things can get tough. There are issues that need resolving, but you don't know how. Employees may have brought up sensitive subjects or engaged in misconduct that's harming the firm's reputation. Some employees aren't performing, and you know who they are. Handling this wrong can cause even more problems, so you're afraid to take the leap, and the problems get worse as they go unaddressed.

But you have to bite the bullet. You have to have these conversations.

Address performance issues or behavioral issues directly but privately. For example, if a team member is underperforming, schedule a one-on-one meeting to discuss their performance, offer support, and set clear expectations moving forward.

Most times, leaders know the decisions they need to make are tough, and it's not just decisions about termination. It could be that someone's just not hitting the mark, or someone said or did something they shouldn't have.

I talked to a manager named Mary, who, for ninety days, was tracking the performance of a sales rep. The rep was nowhere close to hitting their marks, and Mary knew the conversation should've been had ninety days ago. However, Mary was conflicted because the rep had a family to feed too, and she didn't want to ruin his day. The way she saw it, talking to this person wouldn't solve the problem.

I asked her, if talking to him about his poor performance wouldn't solve the problem, what would? He wasn't going to magically start making sales the longer she waited. Still, Mary was reluctant, so I decided we would use data to support the conversation. As the saying goes, men lie, women lie, but numbers never lie. She wouldn't be terminating the sales rep; instead, she'd be setting up a performance plan. She was the leader, and this was part of what leaders did. It might not be in the job description, but it was something that needed to be done.

So instead of berating the sales rep, Mary laid out the data. She pointed out where his goals were, and how far along he was to meeting them. With that, the conversation became much easier. The best part was that the sales rep knew he wasn't hitting his numbers, so he saw the conversation coming. He was expecting to have to talk to the boss.

But it's how you have these difficult conversations that's important. And I always tell leaders to lead with data, talk through the data, then natural conversation will flow. It's not always easy, but oftentimes, the other person expects the conversation anyway.

When Mary laid out the data, she asked the employee what she could do to help him do his job. She found out that the sales rep was doing non-sales work 60 percent of the time, things like service calls and new client onboarding that he shouldn't have been doing. So Mary took those duties off his plate.

Sales increased, and that rep became the sales leader he thought he was going to be when he was hired. But it all started with the conversation—finding out where the challenges were, then fixing those challenges.

The employee can then fulfill their promises. But you've got to fulfill your promises, too. The worst thing you can do is promise too much, then fail to deliver.

Lesson #9: Never Overpromise and Underdeliver

My grandfather always taught me if you say you'll do something, do it.

A lot of the time, we as leaders like to say things we think people want to hear, then we don't do what we said we'd do, or we nitpick over the specifics.

A very specific example of this is my buddy Daniel, who tells the team he will help with continuous learning. He promised everyone that he'd build a world-class learning management system because it's something the team needs. He even promised it would be done in six months. He was very specific about what he was going to do, and he tried to do it all on his own. So instead of building committees within the organization, he overpromised on something he couldn't deliver.

Nine months later, nothing was delivered, and he was rightly called out for it.

Unlike Mary, who had data to support what she was saying, Daniel had no data, no training, and no support to carry out what he said he would, so all he delivered was failure.

A lot of times, we view overpromising and underdelivering from a customer service standpoint. It's bad enough there, but it's worse when it's your employees because they're the ones the customers are talking to and dealing with. The customers will feel as if the company is underdelivering and thus not giving them their money's worth. If you say you'll deliver something in six months, you have to start work right away; you can't put it off until the final thirty days (which is what Daniel did) because then you'll have to work even harder to fulfill your promise, and chances are you can't maintain a grueling pace like that.

To handle this issue, we brought the team in, and Daniel acknowledged that he didn't deliver on what he said he would, and that was a huge deal because accountability was lacking. We were holding him accountable to the six-month timetable. So what he and I did together was ask what critical things needed to be delivered. We then asked the team when they wanted things completed, and the answer was forty-five days.

They were delivered in thirty days.

When we delivered the training the team wanted in a faster turnaround time, the team's success skyrocketed, and we were able to build on those successes. Now, instead of making promises, Daniel asks the team when they want something, then delivers it.

Daniel promised to deliver continuous learning—something you shouldn't neglect.

Lesson #10: Never Neglect Continuous Learning

We're always learning, and we never reach a point at which we know everything there is to know, even if we become experts in a given field. It is always to our benefit to keep learning and keep doing.

Around the time that ChatGPT was getting major buzz and the field of AI was getting major attention for the first time in a long while, the leader of an insurance company—let's call him Bob—worked in the technology department of this company but didn't tell the board of directors about machine learning in the insurance industry. Bob heard all this talk of AI and blew it off, treating it as a fad that would fade into irrelevance in a short time. He'd heard about machine learning and AI before, so he thought that it was just bluster.

But three of Bob's competitors jumped into the machine learning space. This allowed those companies to upgrade their processes and improve their ability to sell policies, all while reducing (though not eliminating) the human workload; what used to take five people now takes one person. Those companies succeeded while Bob's company sank like a stone.

Bob was terminated.

Bob didn't care to update himself on how technology was changing. This is why continuous learning is so important—things do change over time, and you have to stay ahead of the game. Once upon a time, you could never have gotten my mother to store her credit card info on the internet. Now, she won't do business with anyone if she can't pay them online—and she pays quickly.

Times change, and everyone has to change with them, leader or not. The teams we lead are changing. We have to stay up to date with how our industry is changing, whatever that industry is. We have to evolve, adapt, and adjust.

And it all starts with continuous learning.

Learning never stops for a leader. Learning about their people never stops for a leader. You don't want to be like Bob, getting passed by as everything around you transforms. It's better to learn and adapt.

And that way, you can always be a great leader.

10 | How to Bow Out Gracefully

What do you do when the clock turns back? All good leaders were once followers, and many become followers once again. How do you manage that transition well and not fall prey to pride or become consumed by resentment? How you manage that will determine where you go from here on out.

Let's look at the story of Mark, who found himself moving out of his old leadership role.

Mark Passes the Reins

Mark, one of my good friends, had owned a business for more than twenty years. Having put that much time into the business, it was his baby, his pride and joy. But it was also a time of technological change, and with social media on the rise as a vital marketing tool, Mark just didn't have what it took to manage a company that had come up in a very different era.

But Mark struggled with the pride that most leaders have. He figured he could just adapt, but in truth, Mark was never going to change. He could say whatever he wanted, but his team knew he wouldn't change. This business was a marketing agency, and Mark wanted to stay old school in this fast-changing technological environment. He still thought in terms of TV and magazines and newspapers. He still wanted to fax people things. He had to understand that he wasn't going to get clients that way. He wasn't going to grow his business or get new employees like that. And if he couldn't understand that things were different, it was time for someone who could.

So when I spoke with Mark, I asked him, "Mark, do you always try to evolve as you get older and as technology out-consumes you? Or do you want to leave a legacy? Don't you want to be a leader who leaves a lasting legacy?" It was better that he put the legacy first and understood that stepping aside was OK.

So I spent four months working with Mark on how he would announce his exit. We worked not only on what he would say and how he would deliver his speech but also on how he would clarify that he was leaving for good and not coming back to check in. There wasn't going to be this in-between space where he wasn't the boss but was still kind of involved. It was to be a clean separation; he was done.

We built a big story emphasizing Mark's legacy in the company. This way, Mark could still be proud of all he had accomplished as he walked away.

The Point of Leaving

As a leader who is on the way out, you need to bow out with gratitude.

With Mark, that meant thanking his team for all the contributions they made to the company's success—important because it's never about the leader; it's always about the team. You must emphasize that now because that acknowledgement is going to be the lasting image. You've taken the company through its highs and lows, through its successes and its failures, and you leave your leadership position with gratitude for everyone who made your accomplishments possible. You emphasize how your team kept your clients on your side.

They won't just be your final words; they will be your lasting legacy—the thing that motivates the team to keep moving forward and building on everything you've made possible.

But you have to know not only how to feel gratitude but also how to express it and make it part of who you are. You want to feel grateful for everyone who has helped you along the way.

How to Be Grateful

The first thing you should do is a weekly reflection. In this reflection, you should ask, "What am I grateful for?" It's best to do this in some sort of weekly journal (paper or digital) so you can see what it is you don't pay enough attention to.

The next thing is to acknowledge wins and the people who contributed to those wins. Do this on a monthly basis; if that isn't possible, do it on a quarterly basis instead. Say what the wins were, why they were important, what they helped achieve, and where they all lead.

The third thing you should do is seek feedback. Have several sessions in which you're on the spot receiving feedback, not giving it. That feedback is gratitude expressed without an explicit thank-you. You giving other people time to give their feedback is gratitude in and of itself.

But being grateful is only part of it; the next thing you must do is pass the torch.

Passing the Torch

When you pass the torch to someone, that person has to be ready for the task before them. Even if you are no longer managing the company, your shadow—your legacy—will loom large, and your successor will have huge shoes to fill. This will be one of the most important decisions you'll ever make as leader, more important than anything you did actively managing the company.

First, ask yourself, "What are things that, as a leader, I know I'm good at?" You have to ask yourself this because you need to make sure the person you choose is good at those things too. You have to select based on merit, not friendly or familial connections; that said, this person also has to be someone you trust to carry on your vision. Sometimes, you're not passing the torch to one person but to an entire group. Make sure that group is in line with what you want the company to be after you're gone.

The next thing you have to ask is, "What am I weak at?" Who can you find that's strong where you're weak? Because when you pass the torch, you want to leave the organization stronger, in a position that can take on the challenges of tomorrow, not those of yesterday when you were at the helm. Putting someone new in the leadership role will help you address your company's weak spots if you choose correctly.

As for exactly how you leave, it happens one of four ways: death, retirement, promotion, or demotion. Death is obvious, but it need not be a sudden accident or foul play; it could just as easily be a terminal diagnosis that does you in, giving you some time to say your goodbyes. Retirement is by far the most common; it's the typical scenario of the CEO or company president leaving to promote someone in the C-suite to the leadership role. There's also promotion, in which someone who had a leadership role closer to the employees is now moving up to a role that doesn't involve as much direct management. Demotion is the one most people fear, in which they go from a high role to a low one, usually because of some failure on their part.

However you end up leaving, legacy planning allows you to last longer in the leadership role because you've now put someone into place who can carry on the company mission without you being present. As CEO or company president, you wear many hats, and you need to reach the point at which you can fire yourself and keep things moving.

But while you're setting yourself up to be fired, you're also growing yourself at the same time. You're getting "fired" because you're lifting yourself up to reach something greater. In many ways, it's like a promotion.

And stay focused on that positive aspect because the last thing you want to be is resentful.

Avoiding Resentment

Stepping aside is difficult, especially when you've been in that leadership role for a long time. You're confident in your ability to navigate through challenges because you've done it before. You're convinced that the minute you step aside, the minute you let someone else have the reins, everything will burn.

Don't think like that. Instead, have pride.

When you step away with pride, you won't resent that decision. The key here is to step away on a high note, whatever the reason you're stepping away. You want to retire proud. You want to get promoted proud. You want to be proud of the person or group you're putting in your old leadership role. You want to leave on your terms, not be forced out.

The key here is to make the decision before it's made for you. A key part of healthy pride is having control; if you're shoved out the door, there's no control there. That said, leaving a role you've been in for such a long time is uncomfortable. The discomfort is normal—it's a sign you're growing. (It's called "stepping out of your comfort zone" for a reason.) The thing to avoid is not discomfort but ego, which leads to unhealthy resentment.

Ego is saying "Greg can't do this—only I can." Ego is wanting your name plastered everywhere as you're leaving so no one forgets that you and you alone are the reason for the company's success. Ego is taking sole credit for everything that's going well, celebrating yourself without celebrating the team that made everything happen. Ego doesn't allow a graceful exit.

But let's say you do exit. You get out of your old role, and you're happy with your successor. How do you know you've made the right decision?

How do you know you won't have any regrets?

Mitigating Regret

It's OK to have second thoughts about something, but what we want to avoid is regret. Regret feels like we left something incomplete, like we didn't do our best, and we're not focused on the good.

A good way to look at this is through SWOT analysis—strengths, weaknesses, opportunities, and threats. We do this all the time with our jobs or businesses, but we rarely do this kind of analysis on ourselves. If you do the SWOT analysis on yourself, you'll have no regrets because the information is all there. If you do this on a recurring basis, whether that's monthly, quarterly, or semiannually (I wouldn't do it more often than that), and you put forth the effort to make sure you're moving things forward, you'll be able to live with the results.

In my own life, I've moved on from business ideas. I've moved on from team members. I've even stopped a consulting business I once had when I realized that the people I was doing business with at the time were not the kinds of people I wanted to keep doing business with.

When I found myself in that situation, forcing myself to stay in the business when I'd rather be doing anything else, I stayed longer than I should have because I didn't want to be the bad guy. I didn't want to go up to twenty-five people and say "Hey, I don't like you anymore, so scram."

When I did the SWOT analysis, I found that as a business, it was earning a profit, but personally, I was not fulfilled. I considered hiring someone to replace me, but I didn't want to put that person in the same situation I was in. I considered promoting one of my team members, but they were feeling the same thing I was. So I made a tough but necessary decision: I told my twenty-five clients that I wasn't going to renew their contracts. We had gone as far as we could.

I don't hide things from my clients. When we sit down, we talk about all facets of the business. One of the things I put in my contract is that if you're not fit for a leadership position, if you're not fit for growth, if you won't commit to what's required of you, we will have that conversation, and you will be OK with having that conversation per the contract. All leaders have to understand that they might not be best for their team.

But also, there'll be a time when you'll have to promote yourself even though the position you want doesn't exist at the moment.

With one client, the next level of leadership the organization had was executive vice president, as opposed to a C-suite. The current executive vice president was promoted to that position and had no plans to leave, but the person I was advising was ready to leave. So I suggested that this client groom their own replacement. If you can replace yourself, you show that you're ready for promotion, even if the promotion isn't ready for you right now.

I tell my clients not to wait for a position to open up; go create one instead. And in order to do that, you have to replace yourself because you'll be surprised at what the boss or owner will do when you show them that this new person can take your old job. While risky, it's worth it because you've shown you're capable of that. Training your replacement is harder than a lot of people assume. And once you do that, you can leave your old position without regrets.

Knowing how to step away with grace is crucial, but effective leadership also hinges on the choices you make along the way. Up next, we'll dive into the principles of mastering decision-making to navigate challenges and opportunities with precision.

11 | Calm, Cool, Collected: Leading Under Intense Pressure

Nothing tests your ability to lead like a crisis, and COVID-19 was a big one.

I had a client named Rebecca (same Rebecca as earlier), who worked in health care (as you know). Early in the COVID outbreak, no one knew what to do. At this point, we were on month four, and the cases were piling up. We had started working together right before COVID struck, and the suddenness of the outbreak had blindsided us. As the case counts rose, we had to make a decision: How many patients with COVID do we allow? Or do we become a dedicated COVID facility, turning away anyone who didn't have COVID because other diseases didn't take vacations just because COVID was present. So many hospitals had to make that decision; it was difficult to meet the needs of people with non-COVID medical issues.

At this point, the admin staff panicked because two out of every three patients had COVID, and the staff themselves were afraid of catching it. But as the staff panicked, Rebecca did not, though she was stressed. And, in a meeting, I could see it. She was unfocused on what we were talking about, and she had to pause every three minutes to answer a question.

So I asked her to talk to me about what was going on. As she told me about the crisis in her hospital, I told her that she was the leader no matter what. She had to have the cool hand as everything went crazy because if the leader panics, everyone else does, too. By not being the stable voice, she created more chaos. Realizing the implications, she wanted to know how to do that.

Because Zoom wasn't widely used yet, I walked her through this process over the phone. I couldn't make any decisions for her, but I could advise her, and so I did. I explained that there were things she needed to consider.

One: What was the right thing for her community? Two: What was the best thing for her staff? Three: What's best for the business? In a time of crisis, community must come first. Ordinarily, it would be employees, business, then community, but we were in a pandemic, so we had to change the order of priority.

I spent four hours with her on the phone talking about these things, and at the end of the call, she decided that her ER was going to become a dedicated COVID facility. So I said she'd need a partner for non-COVID emergencies. She had two or three resources who could help, so we moved on to planning the internal communication with the team because that was key. And when we worked out how we would communicate with the team, we started with the *because*, not the *why*. We were doing all this because the community needed us. The only silver lining was that the emergencies Rebecca dealt with were not like those in New York City or Chicago, where patients were coming in with gunshot wounds.

As for how Rebecca was to communicate, I told that she had to come in stern because in the midst of chaos, stern matters. Everyone needed to see that she had power, and she was going to dominate the situation. They needed to hear that power coming from her, so she could rally the troops. She had to let everyone know who had to be contacted for what. From there, she told those under her to be stern as well.

Her being a voice of calm filtered down to the team, and she found that with this approach, decision-making was easier than ever. Everyone knew what to do, and the people coming in felt like things were under control. Outside, the pandemic was raging, and everyone was still fumbling through all the problems it caused. But Rebecca's ER was a place of calm, a place where things were being handled. For Rebecca, this was one of the biggest wins of her career—not deciding whether her facility would be COVID or general but developing a plan to handle the crisis and executing that plan successfully. While every day wasn't perfect, she had a plan, so she knew what to do. When you don't have a plan, everything is chaotic, and nothing gets done, but when you do, you can navigate the storm and come out on top.

By managing her stress, Rebecca turned a disaster into a victory. Chances are that you will face many crises in your own career, and the same techniques that helped Rebecca will help you as well.

Being Mindful

The key to being mindful in a crisis is focusing on clear strategic action. You'll never avoid the stress or the fear, but you can reach a point at which you're able to withstand it as you do everything you need to do.

To focus on clear strategic action, you have to take stock of what's on your plate. The reality is that not everything you are burdened with is important; a lot of it is there because you want to feel productive. Thus, the key thing you must do is sideline everything that isn't important, which can be as simple as separating the needs from the wants and focusing only on the needs.

Once you've narrowed things down to your needs, what has priority? Because when you have a full plate, nothing can be added to it. As a leader, things will always be added to what you need to do. Whether you're responsible for those things or not, things will try to get onto your plate. But you won't always have room for this stuff, and this is where all the stress comes from. So I always tell clients they never need a full plate; most of what's on their plates, they don't need to eat.

Another important thing to remember is that crises reveal character. During a crisis, everyone sees who you really are. Leaders who can prove themselves in a crisis are good leaders. A good leader must do their best to manage their hard power when times get tough, meaning they must look after their people and make sure everyone knows what they must do. They not only need to give the orders, but they must also stick to the plan themselves. This careful use of hard power strengthens their soft power just as much, making people more willing to listen to them, even in times of calm.

Ground your mind in the present. Forget about yesterday and forget about next month; worry only about today and the immediate future as you make your way through everything. In these intense situations, clarity is your strongest weapon. Remember that as leader, you're not worrying only about yourself—there are others counting on you. Be that rock, that source of certainty, because when things are going wrong, certainty is what they need.

As the crisis intensifies, so will the stress. That stress isn't your enemy, but letting it control you is. Your job is to take that stress and turn it into focused action. With a crisis afoot, you'll be scared, but it's your job to power through it because the tasks you need to complete won't ease up, no matter how scared you are.

Stop reacting; start planning. Don't wait for things to go wrong because by then it's too late. As the saying goes, failing to prepare is preparing to fail. Things will go wrong, so you have to anticipate the most likely scenarios and come up with ways to get around them. But even so, you might run into something you don't anticipate. While you can't see those coming, that's no excuse not to stay ahead of possible threats. (SWOT analysis comes in handy here.)

Be fine with people throwing stones at you. Not every decision you make is going to be popular, but you don't care about popular; you care about getting things done, especially when everything's going wrong. The normal instinct is to make sure everyone likes you, but you must fight that temptation. When everything's burning, being liked won't help you put the fire out. Furthermore, let the challenges come at you with full force. Each one makes you stronger, sharper, and more prepared. Your resilience under pressure defines you as a leader who doesn't just survive, but thrives.

A Leader's Moment

Crises are moments of truth for leaders. All of a person's qualities are amplified during a crisis, which presents a true picture of a leader's character. Any leader can present themselves as great when times are easy, but only someone who has what it takes can prove capable during hard times. This is how you live out your full potential because this is what reveals it. Show yourself what you're made of when trouble arises because it will. You may not have had a role model for this, but many others may not have either, and you get to be that first role model for leading through crisis, for yourself and for others.

No leader has nailed everything. I'm always working and improving, and you have to do the same. You must continue to evolve and continue to learn more about yourself so you can be the most effective leader. Nobody ever got everything right, but that doesn't mean you can't strive to get *most* things right. And that striving will ultimately take you from leadership beginner level . . . toward mastery. That's when you've gone from learning the fundamentals, to *embodying* them. A leader is who you are. It's not something you "do" anymore. It's as if it's in your DNA. It will be.

12 | Your Leadership DNA

We're going to switch gears a little bit now. Think of what has come before as the fundamentals of this art called leadership. But now, we move you on up—toward mastery. And mastery in leadership is manifest, in my experience and in that of those you've read about so far in this book, in four ways. First let me explain.

Leadership is deeply personal, shaped by your individual traits, experiences, and values. In this chapter, we explore the concept of **Leadership DNA**—your unique combination of strengths, blind spots, and the core qualities that define how you lead. Understanding your personal Leadership DNA helps uncover the essence of your leadership style, offering a personalized approach that resonates with authenticity and purpose.

That said, just as DNA has four chemical bases—A (Adenine), C (Cytosine), G (Guanine), and T (Thymine)—so, too, are there four "base leadership types." You, in all your uniqueness, are going to match one of the four more closely than you match any of the others. I like to call these the **Four Leadership Archetypes** because they supersede all of our unique leadership stories, the story of how we wound up in leadership. Our leadership type describes us similarly to a personality test, but it also *prescribes* us. That is, the archetype can advise us on how to best leverage our uniqueness as people in our position of power. And so the better you become as a leader, *the more you will embody the traits of your archetype*. Isn't that interesting to think about? The more *you* that you become as an authentic leader . . . the more you become just like other authentic leaders of your kind, of your archetype, of your leadership DNA. That is interesting.

Alright now, with that preamble aside, let's review the Four Leadership Archetypes—**Apex Leaders, Ignitor Leaders, Forge Leaders, and Nexus Leaders**—and how these distinct traits influence your ability to inspire and guide others. By assessing your unique traits, you gain clarity on how your leadership style impacts those you lead and how adapting your approach enhances effectiveness. Whether you're seeking to refine your skills or embark on a new leadership journey, this chapter provides the framework to understand and leverage your Leadership DNA for greater influence and impact.

The Four Leadership Archetypes

Leadership comes in many forms, each shaped by unique traits and approaches. Understanding your Leadership DNA helps categorize these styles into distinct archetypes. These Four Leadership Archetypes—Apex Leaders, Ignitor Leaders, Forge Leaders, and Nexus Leaders—reflect the core strengths and behaviors that define how leaders inspire, guide, and create impact—and how they can improve in service of doing all of that. First, we have Apex Leaders.

Apex Leaders

Apex Leaders are visionaries. They thrive on creating a clear, strategic path toward a compelling future. Their strength lies in seeing the bigger picture, setting long-term goals, and inspiring teams with a sense of purpose. Apex Leaders are focused, confident, and decisive. They excel in defining vision, setting direction, and aligning teams toward achieving ambitious outcomes.

Strengths:

- Strategic thinking
- Goal setting and vision creation
- Leading with confidence and purpose

Challenges:

- Can be perceived as too focused on the future, sometimes overlooking immediate team needs
- May struggle with day-to-day operational details

Ignitor Leaders

Ignitor Leaders bring energy and enthusiasm to everything they do. They are driven by passion and thrive in dynamic, fast-paced environments where creativity and innovation are valued. Their ability to ignite enthusiasm motivates teams, sparks progress, and overcomes obstacles. Ignitor Leaders are charismatic, flexible, and quick to adapt to change.

Strengths:

- Inspires with enthusiasm and vision
- Encourages innovation and collaboration
- Adaptable and resilient under pressure

Challenges:

- Can sometimes lack focus on long-term strategy
- Risk of burnout due to high energy output

Forge Leaders

Forge Leaders excel in creating and refining systems, structures, and processes. They are meticulous planners who drive execution with precision. Their ability to build strong frameworks ensures efficiency, reliability, and consistency in operations. Forge Leaders are detail-oriented, organized, and value quality outcomes.

Strengths:

- Excellent at creating structure and order
- Focused on precision and execution
- Strengthens teams through systematic approaches

Challenges:

- May resist change and prefer stability
- Can be overly detail-focused, slowing decision-making

Nexus Leaders

Nexus Leaders are masterful at fostering collaboration and harmony within teams. They create inclusive environments where people feel heard and valued. Their strength lies in uniting diverse perspectives, building relationships, and promoting empathy and understanding. Nexus Leaders are diplomatic, team-focused, and skilled at conflict resolution.

Strengths:

- Builds strong, connected teams
- Promotes collaboration and inclusivity
- Skilled in conflict resolution and fostering trust

Challenges:

- May struggle with delivering decisive action
- Balancing empathy with assertiveness can be difficult

Understanding which archetype resonates most with you provides valuable insights into how you lead and the impact you have on your team. By recognizing your strengths and weaknesses, you can refine your approach and adopt a leadership style that aligns with your values and enhances your effectiveness. (Please note that that adoption does happen consciously. But it will be because you already subconsciously resonate with one of the four more than any of the others.)

Now with the introductions to each out of the way, let's drill down into each specific archetype so you know for sure which you best match—and how to embody those strengths the best in your own life and on your journey to mastering the art of leadership.

13 | The Vision and Strategy of Apex Leaders

Apex Leaders are those who excel in shaping the future through a powerful vision and strategic execution. These leaders possess the ability to see beyond immediate obstacles and craft a compelling vision that guides their teams toward success.

These leaders craft goals with clarity, aligning resources to pave the way forward. They inspire confidence. They maintain focus. Their teams, motivated and united, chase a common goal.

Executing their strategies isn't easy. Balancing ambition with practicality presents its own trials. Adapting to change and overcoming resistance are part of the journey. In this chapter, we'll explore how an Apex Leader manages these hurdles. They create a culture where innovation flourishes. Adaptability becomes second nature. Their leadership drives meaningful outcomes. And this is how they do that—let's meet a client we'll call Marco. Watch and learn.

Learn from the Best: Marco, the Apex Leader

I first met Marco back when he was sketching out plans for what he called "the most visionary retail experience in town." Even then, he had that trademark confidence—the kind that made you believe he could pull off anything he set his mind to. You could see it in the way he talked about growth, expansion, and long-term strategy. He wanted more than just another clothing store with "good quality" and "great prices"; he wanted a space where people felt invited into a future of stylish possibilities.

Marco opened his upscale retail clothing store in a newly developed part of the city, a place known for its chic apartment buildings and trendy restaurants. From the moment the doors swung open, he showed all the signs of being what some call an Apex Leader: he was focused, decisive, and unwavering in his vision. He saw beyond the immediate, always planning several steps ahead. Marco had studied market trends, brought in lines from up-and-coming designers, and planned out brand collaborations that would keep his store on the cutting edge for years to come. And believe me, I admired it all. He had a gift for thinking big and making people see why his ideas mattered.

But with every good eye, there's a blind spot—metaphorically speaking, of course. For Marco, it was the present moment. He got so wrapped up in tomorrow that sometimes he forgot about today—about the staff who were actually running his high-end displays and greeting the shoppers in real time. One day, I stopped by to see how he was doing and noticed that his assistant manager was looking a bit overwhelmed. Boxes were piled up in the back, and a couple of employees were scrambling to figure out the new inventory system Marco had introduced a week earlier. They told me Marco was in his office, huddled over a blueprint for some future location. It was classic Marco—he was always working on the next big thing.

After I managed to chat with him, I brought up what I'd seen in the back. He brushed it off at first. "Yeah, we need to reorganize that stockroom eventually," he said. "But right now, I'm trying to finalize the concept for our second store. I want to position us at the forefront of fashion retail technology." That was the essence of Marco—eyes always on the horizon. But the more we talked, the more it became clear that the team was struggling with day-to-day operations. Shoppers were coming in, but they sometimes left without the level of personal service that Marco claimed was his store's hallmark. It wasn't that he didn't care—he deeply valued his people—but he was so focused on expansion, new trends, and the bigger picture that immediate needs were falling through the cracks.

I saw the same tension arise during a staff meeting where Marco was supposed to walk everyone through a new sales initiative. He started by talking about revenue projections for the next three years, describing how they could become the city's leading fashion brand. It sounded thrilling. He went on and on about the vision, that typical sparkle in his eye, and everyone was on board—until it came time for the day-to-day details. The employees had practical questions: *How would inventory be tracked? Did they have a plan for scheduling floor coverage during peak hours? Who was handling training for these new lines Marco had just introduced?* But Marco's answers were vague. He kept pivoting back to the store's long-range promise. People left the meeting with more enthusiasm for the future but little clarity on how they'd make it happen.

That's when I decided to have a real conversation with him. I said, "Marco, you're brilliant at painting a picture of what comes next. I've never known anyone with your ability to see long-term goals so clearly and rally people around them. But here's the thing: if you never address the realities of right now, you could lose your team before you even get to the future you're envisioning."

He paused—something he rarely did—and let out a slow breath. "I hear you," he said, "but I just feel like if I get bogged down in the details, I'll lose the momentum. I want to be the place everyone's talking about, the store that influences what people wear tomorrow, not just today."

It took a few more conversations, plus some feedback from his most trusted employees, for him to see that no matter how compelling the future might be, the present needed his attention, too. Customers were crucial; staff needed guidance. When I pressed him on how much time he actually spent each day checking in with his employees and making sure operations ran smoothly, he admitted it was far less than he thought. He realized that if the current store faltered, it wouldn't matter how grand his future plans were.

So Marco started making some changes. He restructured his leadership team, creating a role specifically devoted to day-to-day operations. He brought in someone who thrived on detail and process, giving them the authority to handle scheduling, training, and inventory management. This way, Marco could keep his eyes on the horizon while trusting that the immediate needs of the store wouldn't be ignored.

It wasn't easy for him at first. He liked being in control, and handing over responsibilities made him uncomfortable. But as the weeks went on, he saw that having someone else take the reins on daily logistics didn't diminish his vision at all. In fact, it strengthened it. Employees felt supported. Customers noticed that service was more personalized. And Marco was free to spend time on the things he did best: forging new partnerships, scouting fresh designer lines, and brainstorming innovative ways to elevate the in-store experience.

The turning point came during a city-wide fashion event a few months later. The store was buzzing with activity, from high-profile customers to local media outlets. Normally, Marco might have gotten pulled in multiple directions, trying to manage everything on his own. But this time, he had a system in place. His operations lead made sure the staff was well-prepared, inventory was accessible, and checkout lines ran smoothly. Meanwhile, Marco was able to have a lot of fun—greet VIP guests, talk about the brand's philosophy, and generate excitement for the store's upcoming expansions. It was, in a word, successful.

In the aftermath, Marco told me he finally understood that being an Apex Leader wasn't about ignoring the present; it was about uniting the present with the future. "I always believed my job was to paint a vision," he said. "Now I see how crucial it is to let others bring the details to life." His team was more engaged, sales were steadily increasing, and the store had become a favorite spot for local shoppers as well as visitors.

I reminded him of those early days, back when he was still juggling a blueprint in one hand and a lengthy task list in the other. "You haven't lost any of that spark," I told him. "In fact, you've sharpened it, because now your team trusts that you're not leaving them to handle the day-to-day alone."

That's the part that stuck with Marco most. Trust. The team trusted him not only to dream big but also to care about what mattered each day. Marco might not ever be the person who loves dealing with every operational detail—that's just not who he is. But he's learned to respect the necessity of it and to hire people who excel in that realm. In doing so, he's become an even stronger leader.

And in the end, that's the balance Marco had to strike. It wasn't about diminishing his passion for the future; it was about making space for his team to handle the present. The store continued to evolve, eventually expanding into other markets, just as Marco had envisioned. But this time around, he had solid ground under his feet. He wasn't just dreaming—he was building a legacy that could stand the test of time. And that's what Apex Leaders do.

Maybe you're one of them.

14 | The Energy and Momentum of Ignitor Leaders

Ignitor Leaders are dynamic forces in any organization, known for their ability to ignite enthusiasm and drive momentum. They excel at motivating teams, encouraging innovation, and fostering a collaborative atmosphere where creativity thrives.

These leaders understand the importance of setting clear, actionable strategies to guide their teams toward achieving ambitious goals. Balancing their passion with a grounded perspective ensures that enthusiasm is channeled effectively, even when faced with pressure and resistance.

By skillfully navigating challenges and keeping their teams aligned, Ignitor Leaders create a culture of sustained success and growth. Let's meet one of them, a client we'll call Laquesha.

Learn from the Best: Laquesha, the Ignitor Leader

I remember the first time I met Laquesha. She was bouncing from one treadmill to the next, offering quick tips to the women huffing away on their morning runs. Every so often, she'd break away to correct someone's squat form near the weight rack or demonstrate a new band workout she'd just discovered. What struck me right off the bat was her energy—like a spark that never went out, even when everyone else had drained their last bit of stamina. It was no surprise, then, when she mentioned her plan to open her own gym. The place she was working at was too small for her dreams, she said, and she wanted to do more than just train clients one-on-one. She wanted a space where everyone could feed off that energy and push themselves further than they ever thought possible.

Not many people can pull off a transition from personal trainer to gym owner. But Laquesha was different: an Ignitor Leader to her core. She didn't just sell workout programs—she sold the vision that each session could be transformative, that the hustle and sweat would lead to real and lasting change. When an opportunity arose to buy a larger facility on the other side of town, she jumped in with both feet. The building needed some TLC, but you couldn't tell Laquesha anything once her mind was set. The next thing I knew, she was painting walls, installing new treadmills, and hiring staff to help her manage the influx of clients who trickled in, curious to see what all the buzz was about.

At first, she mostly stuck to what she knew: personalized fitness programs, high-energy group classes, and a focus on uplifting the women who had been her core clientele from the start. But as word spread, men started showing up too, lured by the promise of a dynamic, inspiring environment. Her gym became a community hub where people from all walks of life could meet, train, and swap stories about sets, reps, and weekend meal prep. Laquesha thrived in that setting—she'd greet new members at the door with a grin so genuine it was contagious, then bounce back to a group class to lead a quick, improvised circuit training routine if the instructor had to step out.

However, like any Ignitor Leader, her gift for generating momentum sometimes overshadowed the necessity of having a solid, long-term strategy. One day, I was sitting in her office—really just a corner of the break room with a desk and a whiteboard—when she started scribbling new ideas. She wanted to expand the class schedule, add child-care services, and maybe even set up an outdoor training area for warm-weather boot camps. Each idea sounded fantastic on its own, but it was all a bit scattered. One of her senior trainers finally spoke up, saying, "Laquesha, I love the passion. But what's the plan for making all this happen?"

That was the moment she realized she needed to step back from the whirlwind of creativity and think about how she'd actually execute these ideas. She asked me to help her outline the next few steps, from hiring new staff to redesigning the floor plan to accommodate more equipment. It wasn't that she lacked the ability—far from it. She just needed a little prompting to sit still for more than a minute and figure out how to turn her energy into concrete objectives.

Over the next few weeks, we worked on structuring her thoughts into what she called a "growth blueprint." She drafted SMART goals for membership numbers, mapped out a timeline for remodeling, and even considered launching an online platform for remote coaching. But she never lost that spark. Even while planning, she'd jump up mid-sentence to demonstrate a new routine she was concocting in her head. Her staff joked that all their best brainstorming sessions happened in workout gear because there was no telling when Laquesha would decide a "quick demonstration" was in order.

Still, with all her energy, there were times she risked burnout. She'd be at the gym from dawn until late into the night, working with early-bird clients and staying long after closing to review finances or fix a broken elliptical. One evening, her assistant manager, a calm and methodical guy named Terry, found her collapsed on a yoga mat, half-asleep. She'd been running on pure adrenaline for weeks, pulling double duty as owner and lead trainer, plus trying to mentor a new batch of instructors she'd hired. Terry suggested she delegate some responsibilities for the sake of her own health. At first, Laquesha resisted—she was used to being the one who fired everyone up, who set the tone and pace for the entire gym. But she knew he was right. If she ran herself into the ground, the whole place would suffer.

That conversation prompted her to reorganize her team. She appointed a head of operations to handle day-to-day scheduling, equipment maintenance, and membership inquiries. She also shifted her primary focus to mentorship: training her trainers. Every Wednesday morning, she held a staff workshop, where she'd challenge them to come up with new exercises or group class formats. "Bring the spark," she'd say. "Show me something I've never seen before!" The trainers loved it—it was a chance to innovate without fear of judgment, and Laquesha was always their biggest cheerleader.

Clients started noticing a difference. Not only was Laquesha still her radiant, energetic self, but the entire gym environment seemed turbocharged with creativity. One corner of the facility became a sort of test lab for new workout ideas. A trainer who specialized in Pilates blended it with high-intensity interval training. Another who loved dance integrated Latin rhythms into a core-strengthening routine. None of these ideas came from a mandatory assignment; they stemmed from the environment Laquesha had cultivated—one where experimentation was welcomed, and collaboration was the norm.

Of course, not everyone responded well to change. A handful of longtime members grumbled about the noise or the unconventional workouts that spilled into the main gym floor. Some felt the gym was losing its simpler, more personal vibe. Laquesha listened carefully. She recognized that not everyone shared her appetite for novelty, and she worked with Terry to create "quiet zones" for those who preferred more traditional workouts. By validating their concerns and providing alternatives, she turned potential resentment into understanding. Even if they didn't love every new addition, they appreciated that Laquesha respected their needs.

And that's how she handled most pressure and resistance: head-on and with empathy. If a trainer was struggling to keep up with the pace, she'd invite them for a one-on-one talk. She had a knack for making people feel comfortable enough to voice doubts and insecurities. "We're all on this journey together," she'd say, "and I want you to shine in your own way." She was never short on reassuring words, but she also knew when to be firm. If someone repeatedly fell short on responsibilities, she didn't hesitate to have that difficult conversation. She believed in second chances—but she also believed that the energy of the gym depended on every member of the team pulling their weight.

Within a year, Laquesha's gym had doubled in membership. People from all over the city came in droves, attracted by the stories of an owner who made exercise feel like a party—but also ensured that results were real. Her Wednesday workshops became legendary among local trainers, many of whom applied just for a chance to learn from her.

I asked her once how she managed to keep that flame alive. She told me it wasn't just about having energy; it was about sharing it. "If I just keep the spark to myself," she explained, "I'll burn out. But if I spread it around, it becomes a collective thing. That's how this place thrives." And she was right. That unique blend of passion, collaboration, and adaptability is what made her gym so special. Laquesha's story proved that an Ignitor Leader can build a culture where enthusiasm isn't just a buzzword—it's the driving force behind real, tangible success. And if you're an Ignitor Leader, you'll create that in your people, too.

15 | The Structure and Precision of Forge Leaders

Forge Leaders are driven by a commitment to structure, precision, and creating systems that promote long-term success. These leaders excel in maintaining consistency, enhancing operational efficiency, and adapting their approach to meet evolving needs.

In today's ultra-rapidly changing business environment, where precision and adaptability are crucial as tomorrow's headlines are seemingly the opposite of yesterday's, Forge Leaders stand out for their ability to balance order with innovation. They understand that strong foundations and well-defined processes are essential for sustainable growth.

Let's see how Forge Leaders cultivate discipline, foster adaptability, and drive results through strategic, structured approaches. This is the story of another client, Harris.

Learn from the Best: Harris, the Forge Leader

It was a sunny Monday afternoon at the mall. Small crowds were seeping in for lunch and some quick shopping. And there was Harris. I'd met him at a networking event locally, and I hadn't yet seen his space. He was standing by the front desk of his newly acquired barbershop, quietly watching the cadence of customers with a focused, barberly intensity.

Harris had told me a little about himself when we first met. Earlier in his career, he'd been just one of the barbers cutting hair in that very space. But he was an owner now, and he looked like it. Owning an eight-chair barbershop in a rare bustling mall was no small feat, and he seemed determined to get every detail right.

There's a little more about Harris that you should know. In the five years he'd worked as a barber, he'd often be the last one there each night, wiping down the stations and making sure the clippers were cleaned and organized. While other barbers chatted about weekend plans or the latest sports scores, Harris meticulously recorded inventory of combs, blades, and other supplies. It was just how he was wired—methodical, precise, and unwilling to let small details slip through the cracks. That's what set him apart as a Forge Leader: the ability to build strong systems and maintain high standards day in and day out.

When the former owner decided to retire, Harris was the natural choice to take over. He knew the shop's clientele, had a vision for streamlining operations, and above all, understood what made a haircut a great experience for customers. Still, transforming himself from a solitary barber into a manager and owner of an entire shop came with its own hurdles. He no longer spent his days behind a chair with a comb and scissors in hand; instead, he had to organize schedules, manage supply chains, and ensure that each barber followed a uniform set of standards.

One of the first things he did was create a detailed operations manual. He wrote down everything—how to greet a customer, how to sanitize stations properly, even guidelines for background music. Some of the more experienced barbers rolled their eyes. They'd been cutting hair for years, and they knew what they were doing. "We don't need a manual for greeting a customer," one of them said with a half-laugh. But Harris stayed calm and explained that with the foot traffic the mall brought in, consistency was key. "If we're going to handle this many walk-ins, we need to be consistent with every single person who sits in our chairs," he insisted. "That's how we keep them coming back."

And he was right. Within a few weeks, the barbers came around when they saw how much smoother the operation ran. Instead of each person winging it, there was a clear process. Customers were greeted promptly, asked their preference (whether they had a favorite barber or needed the next available), and got a clean smock without fail. The waiting area never piled up with confused customers anymore; everything felt orderly, and reviews started pouring in online about how efficient and clean the shop was. Harris had effectively translated his attention to detail into a system that elevated the entire customer experience.

But building strong frameworks can sometimes make it harder to embrace change. A few months into Harris's ownership, the mall management approached him with an opportunity to collaborate on a weekend promotional event. It involved offering quick, discounted trims near the food court for passersby—an idea that could drive more customers to his shop afterward.

Harris hesitated. He worried that stepping outside the shop's set processes might cause chaos. What if the barbers struggled with portable equipment? How would he manage sanitation and consistent service away from their usual setup?

Eventually, with some encouragement from a neighboring store owner, Harris decided to give it a shot. He drew up a detailed plan for how to transport the necessary tools, how each barber would rotate between the event station and the shop, and even how they'd handle payments. When the weekend event came, it ran like clockwork. People lined up for quick trims, then followed the signs back to the shop for a full haircut or beard trim. They loved the convenience, and he picked up a slew of new customers who hadn't realized his barbershop even existed.

Seeing how a well-thought-out system could adapt when needed was an eye-opener for Harris. It reinforced what he already knew deep down—that structure was essential, but it shouldn't be rigid. Being a Forge Leader wasn't just about implementing standard operating procedures; it was also about refining them when business needs or market trends shifted.

Harris's next step was to adopt some technology to streamline bookings and inventory. He researched various systems, tested them out meticulously, and finally settled on a point-of-sale platform that also tracked product sales and allowed for online appointment scheduling. It took some of the older barbers a bit of time to adjust—typing in customer info and preferences instead of scribbling them on scraps of paper felt foreign. But Harris introduced mandatory training sessions, walking everyone through how to set up an appointment in the system, how to record a sale for styling products, and even how to split tips fairly at the end of the day.

At first, there was a small mutiny brewing. A few barbers complained the system slowed them down, especially with long lines of walk-ins during peak hours. Harris, however, stuck to his plan but stayed open to feedback. He organized a meeting where each barber could voice their frustrations. Then, he methodically addressed each concern: he showed them shortcuts on the platform, simplified the form fields, and even hired a part-time receptionist during weekend rush hours to make sure the barbers could focus on cutting hair instead of data entry. Gradually, the same barbers who had grumbled about the new system started admitting it made their lives easier—no more double bookings, and no more confusion about who was next in line.

Perhaps the strongest testament to Harris's style was how he handled employee performance issues. In a high-traffic mall barbershop, each barber's speed and skill level can vary drastically, and that can affect overall customer satisfaction. One barber, Sam, consistently ran behind on his appointments. He was great with styling, but he'd always get chatty, which led to longer wait times and some unhappy customers. Rather than simply telling Sam to "hurry up," Harris sat down with him and reviewed exactly how many minutes each type of service should take. They timed Sam's haircuts together and pinpointed where he could be more efficient—like prepping his tools in advance or moving the conversation along while trimming instead of pausing every time he spoke.

It was a blend of empathy and structure. Harris recognized Sam's strengths—customers loved his personality—so he didn't want to quash that. But he knew the shop had to maintain a standard to keep people flowing in and out happily. So they agreed on a timeline for improvement and set up weekly check-ins. By the end of the month, Sam had cut his average appointment time by nearly ten minutes, and client satisfaction went up.

Over time, Harris's barbershop became known not just for solid haircuts but for a level of professionalism and efficiency that stood out in an industry where chaos can easily take over. He introduced advanced booking for those who preferred appointments, while still catering to walk-ins with a well-managed queue. He ensured that the shop was fully stocked every morning, each station had a consistent layout, and every barber had a clear understanding of their responsibilities. Yet, within that framework, he gave them the freedom to let their individual personalities shine. It was a careful balance of precision and autonomy, and it worked.

When I asked him what he was most proud of, he said it was the fact that the barbershop ran smoothly even on days when he wasn't around. "That's the mark of a good system," he told me, glancing around at the hustle and bustle of a busy Saturday afternoon. Chairs were filled, barbers were moving swiftly, and customers looked relaxed. "I built something that can stand on its own, whether I'm holding the clippers or not." And that's exactly who Harris was: a Forge Leader who believed that the foundation of success lay in the systems he painstakingly created and refined—so the place could thrive every single day. So can yours, too, when you're a Forge Leader.

16 | The Trust and Collaboration of Nexus Leaders

Nexus Leaders are the linchpins of modern organizations, cultivating trust and fostering collaboration to drive innovation and success. In the modern world's interconnected, international workplace, fostering strong relationships and building collaborative teams are essential for achieving organizational goals big and small.

So, this chapter is going to cover the strategies that Nexus Leaders use to navigate conflicts, enhance communication, and ensure seamless alignment across teams, creating an environment where trust and collaboration thrive.

Through these key approaches, leaders empower their teams to work cohesively, enabling growth and adaptability in a dynamic business landscape. Leaders like Franklin.

Learn from the Best: Franklin, the Nexus Leader

I met Franklin back when he was still juggling every aspect of his fledgling law practice on his own. He was just a solo attorney, struggling to keep up with a rising tide of paperwork and case deadlines. What struck me immediately was how he never seemed frazzled or impatient, even when the phone rang off the hook or a paralegal knocked on his door for the tenth time that hour. Instead, he had this calm, open presence about him—like no matter how busy he got, he had all the time in the world to listen. It was one of those intangible qualities that made people trust him right away.

Over the next few years, Franklin's small practice expanded into a modest but bustling intellectual property (IP) and contract law firm. Patents, trademarks, licensing deals—he took them all on, and his client list began to grow faster than he could keep up with on his own. It didn't take long for him to realize he needed help, not just an assistant or two, but a real team of paralegals who could share the workload and bring their own strengths to the table. And so he hired a handful of bright, eager minds, each bringing a unique perspective on how best to tackle the firm's increasing demands.

From day one, Franklin made it clear that he wanted them all to feel like equals at the table. While he was undoubtedly the firm's star attorney—earning glowing praise for his skill in patent applications and his knack for crafting airtight contracts—he never brandished that status over anyone. Whenever a big client walked in, Franklin introduced each paralegal by name, highlighting their specific expertise. "This is Georgina," he'd say. "She's brilliant at dissecting prior art references, so she'll help us dodge any nasty surprises with your patent." Or, "Meet Samuel—he's a wiz with trademark searches." You could see each paralegal light up with pride at being recognized for their contribution.

It wasn't just lip service. Franklin genuinely wanted a team dynamic that felt inclusive and collaborative. He set up a Monday meeting ritual that everyone quickly embraced: each person would share one success from the previous week and one challenge they currently faced. Georgina might mention struggling with a stubborn client who refused to provide requested documents on time. Samuel might highlight a trademark filing that had been unexpectedly rejected. Franklin listened intently to it all, jotting down notes in a little leather-bound notebook he kept with him at all times.

What stood out in these meetings was how Franklin managed to gently guide without dictating. When Georgina felt overwhelmed, he wouldn't just bark instructions at her. He'd ask, "What options do you see right now?" or "How can the rest of us support you?" That approach was a hallmark of his Nexus Leader style: he aimed to unite people, draw out their perspectives, and create a space where every voice carried weight. He never imposed a single, top-down solution. Instead, he'd build consensus, weaving together different ideas until they settled on a plan that felt right to everyone.

Of course, collaboration isn't always straightforward. One of the paralegals, Terrence, had a more competitive streak than the rest. He came from a larger firm where the culture rewarded individual achievements over team efforts, and it showed in how he handled tasks. Terrence often preferred to work in isolation, hoarding information to make himself look indispensable. He also had a habit of brushing off suggestions or disagreements as if they were personal challenges to his competence.

Before long, tensions rose. Georgina complained that she couldn't finalize certain documents because Terrence wouldn't share crucial updates he'd received from a client. Samuel felt blindsided when Terrence scheduled an in-person meeting with a client they both served, neglecting to even mention it until the eleventh hour. It was the kind of conflict that could easily simmer under the surface and poison a team's morale.

Franklin noticed the tension and decided to address it head-on—but in a way that preserved relationships rather than damaging them. He called Terrence into his office, not for a stern lecture, but to ask open-ended questions. "How are you feeling about your workload?" he ventured. "Is there anything about our team process that isn't working for you?" Terrence, initially defensive, eventually admitted that he found it hard to trust others with information. He'd always been taught to stand out from the crowd by being the best-prepared person in the room, and sharing details felt like giving away his edge.

Instead of scolding, Franklin empathized. "I understand where you're coming from," he said. "But in this firm, our success is measured by how well we function together. Clients come to us because we combine our strengths. If we silo information, we can miss critical details that hurt the client and, by extension, our reputation as a team." He then offered Terrence a real solution: "What if we arrange a quick daily touch-base, just five minutes, to ensure everyone's updated on new intel? You'll still be leading your tasks, but it gives the rest of us a chance to stay in the loop."

Terrence agreed, somewhat warily, but within a week, the daily touch-base became a surprisingly smooth habit. He realized that sharing didn't diminish his worth; it actually elevated the entire team's performance, which made him look even better in front of clients. A subtle shift in attitude took place as he recognized the benefits of open communication. Over time, Terrence began to approach Georgina or Samuel proactively with updates, and the tension that once loomed over the office receded into the background.

Still, Franklin's collaborative approach sometimes led to other challenges. He struggled on occasion with making tough calls, especially when he wanted to preserve harmony. For instance, when a high-profile client demanded a near-impossible turnaround time on a patent filing, the paralegals were split on whether to outsource some of the drafting to a contract service. Half the team felt outsourcing might compromise quality and cause more work later; the other half argued they'd be too swamped to meet the deadline without it. Franklin heard them all out, trying to find a middle ground. Days passed, tension mounted, and the deadline loomed.

In the end, Georgina finally asked him, "Franklin, what are we going to do? We need a decision." He realized he had to pivot from consensus-builder to leader. Gathering the team, he stated plainly, "We're going to handle this in-house. It means long nights, but I trust our process. If we need extra hours, I'll pitch in myself. Let's do a check-in every evening at six to see where we stand." The paralegals might not have unanimously agreed with the call, but they respected that Franklin made it decisively, clarifying the path forward. His empathy and desire for consensus remained intact, but in that moment, he also showed the firm that he knew when to stand firm and provide a definitive direction.

Those hectic weeks were a turning point. Although everyone was tired—some nights leaving well after midnight—they also felt a renewed sense of unity. Franklin didn't just sign off on the final documents; he rolled up his sleeves and worked side by side with each paralegal, reviewing paragraphs, double-checking citations, and ensuring the filing was airtight. The client was beyond thrilled with the speed and thoroughness, and the paralegals, once they finally had a chance to breathe, said they'd never felt more connected as a team.

I remember asking Franklin later how he balanced empathy and assertiveness. He admitted it was an ongoing process. "I think the key is to listen first," he told me, "and truly validate where everyone's coming from. But eventually, you have to weigh all that information and make a call. People want to feel heard, but they also need a leader who can guide them out of a stalemate."

He also touched on how much he valued trust-building. "Trust isn't just about me trusting them," he explained. "It's about them trusting each other, and themselves, too. When everyone knows we have each other's backs, the conflicts don't become personal. They become puzzles we figure out together."

In the months that followed, Franklin continued refining that culture of collaboration. He instituted weekly training sessions where paralegals took turns teaching the rest of the team about a niche area they excelled in. If Georgina discovered a new method for categorizing prior art references, she'd host a mini-seminar. If Terrence found a more efficient way to manage docket deadlines, he'd do the same. Not only did these sessions broaden everyone's skill set, but they also gave each paralegal a moment to shine, boosting both knowledge and morale.

Word got around, and soon enough, Franklin's firm became known in the local legal community for its warm, team-focused atmosphere. Junior attorneys from bigger firms sometimes reached out to see if Franklin was hiring, citing stories they'd heard about how supportive and close-knit his office was. Even clients took notice. Many of them commented on how they always felt like they had an entire "mini family" of legal support, rather than a single overworked lawyer and a few faceless assistants.

That sense of belonging and shared purpose became Franklin's hallmark—he showed that a Nexus Leader could stand at the helm of a high-stakes law practice without forgoing empathy and teamwork. He proved that true harmony in an office didn't have to conflict with productivity or ambition. Quite the opposite: by fostering open lines of communication, encouraging mutual respect, and stepping in decisively only when necessary, Franklin created a workplace where everyone felt valued and motivated to succeed.

In the end, his small IP and contract law firm thrived not just because Franklin was a brilliant attorney but because he was a leader who understood that uniting diverse perspectives can spark real innovation—and, perhaps most importantly, lasting trust. It was a testament to the power of collaboration, empathy, and the willingness to make tough calls when the moment demanded. And if you ask me, that's exactly what a Nexus Leader is all about. You just might be one, too.

17 | The Single Most Critical Insight for Mastering Leadership

If you've read this far, you know that leadership isn't a destination—it's a series of choices. You've seen stories of people who lead by vision, those who spark teams with contagious energy, those who forge rock-solid systems, and those who unite diverse groups with empathy and diplomacy. You've learned that each leader's style can illuminate a unique path to success. But if there's one insight that pulls everything together—one unifying truth that makes mastery of leadership truly possible—it's this:

> **You are the leader, but leadership isn't for you; it's for those you lead.**

This overarching truth might sound simple, but it requires an ongoing shift in how you see yourself, your team, and your goals. So let's break down the different facets of this core insight, showing why it's the most important thing to internalize if you want to master the art of leading as you begin or continue your own journey.

You Are a Steward, Not the Star

In our culture, we often celebrate the lone hero, that superstar celebrity CEO genius who "did it all" or the sports captain who single-handedly snatches victory from defeat. But reality is always more complex. A healthy organization functions because of many interdependent parts—smart planning, consistent processes, genuine relationships, and a shared vision. You might be the central figure orchestrating those parts, but the moment you start seeing yourself as the star who outshines everyone else, you risk undercutting the very team you're supposed to serve.

Stewardship is a commitment to the health and success of something bigger than yourself—a department, a community, or a business mission. You're entrusted with resources, opportunities, and a team of people who have their own hopes and aspirations. Think back to Harris, the barbershop owner who meticulously built out detailed procedures so his business could run as smoothly without him as it did with him. He didn't want to be the star whose name appeared on every success. He wanted a strong, sustainable system that brought out the best in every barber.

When you see yourself as a steward, you become the one removing obstacles, not creating them. You empower others to shine in their own right rather than remain in your shadow. That's the difference between someone who craves the spotlight and someone who builds a stage for everyone to perform at their best.

Team Before Spotlight

Your purpose is to facilitate growth—both the kind that shows up in profits or metrics and the kind that shows up in people's confidence and expertise. Marco, the visionary store owner, discovered that a gorgeous brand image and ambitious expansion plans weren't enough if he neglected the here-and-now needs of his team. It took some gentle confrontations for him to realize that nobody was going to keep stepping up if he stayed laser-focused on tomorrow and brushed aside the pressures of today.

As a leader, you must be vigilant about how your ego might show up. The reason many leaders struggle is not a lack of technical or strategic skill; it's an unwillingness to share credit or a fear of losing status if they're not always in control. Yet the paradox is that the more you elevate your team, the more they elevate you. When individuals feel (and, of course, actually *are*) empowered, heard, and recognized, they don't just meet expectations—they exceed them. And that reflects well on you in the long run.

Feedback Is Your Best Friend

Remember when Chris, the insurance agency owner, found he wasn't engaging customers on social media the way he had expected? He initially thought the problem was the market, the algorithms, or the staff he had hired. But a deeper look revealed that he hadn't asked for feedback in the right ways, nor did he create a structure that allowed his team to shape the marketing strategy with their own ideas.

Nothing kills leadership momentum like ignoring or dismissing feedback. It's easy to believe you have all the answers, especially if you're the one in charge. But here's the real secret: feedback is how you correct your blind spots. Because you can't fix what you can't see. And the more powerful you become—title, rank, or credibility in your organization—the less likely people are to volunteer uncomfortable truths unless you specifically ask for them.

To master leadership, create routines and spaces that invite feedback—weekly one-on-ones, monthly check-ins, or even anonymous surveys. Yes, you'll occasionally hear things you wish you didn't. But if you respond with curiosity rather than defensiveness, you'll spark genuine growth. A team that feels safe giving feedback is one that helps you lead more effectively.

Conflict Means Growth

Most of us shy away from conflict. I sure do. You might, too. See, I worry it will destabilize the team, lead to hurt feelings, or derail projects. But it doesn't, not when managed well. Capable leaders don't worry about conflict because why would they?

Franklin, the diplomatic attorney who built a small law firm into a tight-knit group, encountered conflict that could have festered into resentment and hidden agendas. But instead of sweeping it under the rug, he addressed it head-on, offering real solutions in the form of quick daily "touch-base" meetings and clarifying responsibilities.

What if Franklin had ignored those tensions? The friction between Terrence and the other paralegals might have led to high turnover or poor client satisfaction. Instead, confronting the issue with empathy turned it into an opportunity for the entire team to strengthen communication and trust.

Conflict is rarely the real issue; it's often a symptom that something else is off—a miscommunication, misaligned goals, or different work styles that need some bridging. Leading well means seeing conflict for what it is—a chance to deepen understanding, refine processes, and build a more cohesive team.

Vision Needs Action

Leadership mastery often involves reconciling two seemingly contradictory ideas: you have to dream big like an Apex Leader, but you also have to manage daily tasks with the meticulousness of a Forge Leader. Look at Laquesha, the gym owner brimming with ideas and enthusiasm. She lit a fire under everyone who walked through her doors, but she also risked burning herself out. Only when she paired her raw energy with structured planning did her gym truly flourish.

In essence, big-picture thinking without practical steps is fantasy. Plans and processes without creativity or excitement can become stale. To truly master leadership, you must learn to navigate the dance between vision and reality—knowing when to charge ahead with bold initiatives and when to slow down and anchor them in meticulous strategy.

One practical way is to schedule intentional "vision time," where you map out grand ambitions and "execution time," where you handle the nitty-gritty. If you find yourself leaning too far toward one side, delegate or partner with someone who excels in the other. The best leaders don't try to do everything—they cultivate collaboration that complements their strengths.

The Strongest Mindset Is Resilience

Sooner or later, every leader faces storms—unexpected downturns, cultural shifts, or economic squeezes. You might recall how Rebecca, the health-care leader, had to turn her ER into a dedicated COVID facility practically overnight. She could have panicked or gone into denial. Instead, she grounded herself in a methodical action plan. By balancing care for her team with the urgent needs of her community, she showcased resilience under extreme pressure.

A resilient mindset doesn't mean you're unshakeable; it means you know how to recalibrate when shaken. You can do this by:

1. Acknowledging the crisis: Denial wastes valuable time.
2. Gathering accurate information: You can't plan off rumors.
3. Involving the right people: Collective wisdom often trumps going solo.
4. Communicating consistently: Steady updates keep everyone aligned.
5. Allowing room for empathy: People are at their best when they feel safe and heard.

The ability to pivot, adapt, and keep your team anchored in a shared sense of purpose will define your leadership legacy, especially in turbulent times.

Serve Before Demanding

Religious communities in America talk a lot about "servant leadership," but that's more than just a buzzword or a style. It's an orientation: you, as a leader, exist to serve the mission, the team, and the community you're a part of. When you prioritize service, you automatically consider how policies, decisions, and even small day-to-day choices affect those around you. That filter keeps your ego in check.

Madison, the marketing manager who had a high employee turnover, had to learn to infuse purpose into her team's day to day. When she switched from a top-down, numbers-driven approach to a more empathetic, purpose-driven style—asking team members to articulate their own "because statements"—she noticed a remarkable shift. By setting aside her ego and focusing on *their* motivations, *their* challenges, she became more influential than she ever was through rigid goal setting alone.

A leader who serves first makes everyone feel they matter. That sense of inclusion doesn't feel more than nice; it drives engagement, creativity, and loyalty. And that feels *good*.

Stay True to Your Core

You've encountered the four archetypes: Apex, Ignitor, Forge, and Nexus. It's normal to resonate strongly with one. You might be the big-picture visionary, the dynamic motivator, the systematic operator, or the empathetic connector. Whatever your default style, lean into it. It's where you'll be most naturally impactful.

But **don't stop there.** Every archetype has weaknesses it must compensate for. Apex Leaders risk neglecting details; Ignitor Leaders risk fizzling out after bursts of enthusiasm; Forge Leaders can cling to structure at the cost of innovation; Nexus Leaders may hesitate when decisiveness is needed. Mastery means borrowing strategies from the other archetypes when a situation demands it.

Embrace the synergy of these archetypes: partner with people who fill your gaps, outsource tasks that don't match your gift zone, or challenge yourself to strengthen an area where you're weak. By blending the best of each archetype's mindset, you'll become more adaptable and effective.

Evolve

You've heard it again and again: leadership is a journey, not a fixed identity. The moment you decide you've "arrived" is the moment you start to stagnate. Whether it's Bob, who overlooked an AI revolution in the insurance industry, or Mark, who clung to outdated marketing methods, leaders who refuse to evolve find themselves replaced or irrelevant.

Continuous learning can take many forms. It might be industry-specific—like adopting new technologies—or it might be interpersonal, such as improving your communication or conflict resolution skills. It could be personal growth, like developing emotional intelligence or resilience. The point is that the marketplace, technology, and social norms never stand still, so neither should you.

Schedule personal reviews. Ask your team for honest feedback on your leadership style. Attend seminars, read widely, or immerse yourself in new experiences that stretch you. If you've modeled the willingness to adapt, your team will follow suit.

Own Everything

The final angle of this all-important insight is about **ownership**—not necessarily (just) of the company, but of the outcomes your decisions create. If you can define leadership in a single statement, it would be "the acceptance of responsibility for bringing about positive change." Ownership means you don't just point fingers; you drive solutions. You don't just observe problems; you actively orchestrate improvements.

Ownership also frees you from waiting on permission or perfect conditions. A true leader navigates the environment as it is and harnesses resources creatively to achieve goals. Even if you're not the top-level executive, you can lead from where you are. In fact, you probably already do. The shift that mastery requires is to fully embrace that you have the capacity to create change—right now, with your current resources and constraints.

You see, leadership mastery hinges on your capacity to recognize that your power exists to elevate others. It's a cycle: your vision, your people, and your systems feed into each other. Each success story—from Mark stepping down gracefully to Marco focusing on present operations, from Laquesha igniting progress in her gym to Franklin building trust in his law office—stems from leadership that fosters a healthy environment where everyone thrives. And that's why you're here, and it's what you'll do next. I can't wait to hear how you became a good leader!

What's Next?

Leadership is a journey of constant growth and self-discovery. Strive to learn, evolve, and get better every day. While nobody gets everything right, you can aim to get most things right—and that's where real progress happens.

To continue this journey, join our community at community.mickunplugged.com. Access tools like the Energy Management Workbook and Daily Reflections Workbook, connect with fellow leaders facing similar challenges, and even join a mastermind group or work with my team directly. Step up now, embrace your potential, and become the leader you were born to be.

Tell Me What You Think

Let other readers know what you thought of *How to Be a Good Leader When You've Never Had One*. Please write an honest review for this book on your favorite online bookshop.

About the Author

Michael "Mick" Hunt is the voice and face of modern leadership. He is the host of Mick Unplugged, among the top three self-improvement, top five education, and top one hundred overall podcasts in the world. Mick is also a highly in-demand motivational speaker for the Fortune 500 and top universities, with audiences as large as fifteen thousand, and is the host, emcee, and opening speaker of the Les Brown Power Tour. Mick is a leadership trainer and executive coach to the world's elite leaders and personalities in business, entertainment, education, and government. He is also a member of the Forbes Coaches Council and Forbes Business Council. Meet Mick at www.mickhuntofficial.com.

Index

A

Abstract communication, 83–84
Action:
  in crises, 136, 137
  vision followed by,
    91–92, 98, 175
Adversity:
  finding your role and
    because in, 1–6
  leading in times of, *see* Crisis
    leadership
America, founding of, 92
Apex Leaders:
  embracing synergy of, 177
  strengths and challenges
    for, 141
  vision and strategy of, 145–150
Archetypes of leadership,
  139–143. *See also*
    individual archetypes
  Apex Leaders, 141
  Forge Leaders, 142
  Ignitor Leaders, 141–142
  Nexus Leaders, 142–143

strengths and
  weaknesses of, 177
Asking the right questions, 77
Assured communication, 81–83
Astor, Bill, 117
Attention to detail:
  disguising micromanagement
    as, 44–45
  by Forge Leaders, 159
Authority:
  perception of, 95
  speaking with, 84–85, 88

B

Bad leaders. *See also* Great
  leaders
  communication by, 85–87
  lack of empathy in, 50–52
  micromanagement by, 44–45
  misperception of
    dictatorship by, 45–46
  over-delegation by, 48–49
  self-deception by, 42–44
  self-promotion by, 46–48

187

Balance:
  for Apex Leaders, 150
  of autonomy and oversight, 77
  for Forge Leaders, 157
  of hands-on with oversight, 72–73
  of hard and soft power, 34–35
  for Ignitor Leaders, 151
  for Nexus Leaders, 168
Because, 3, 53–63
  finding your, 7
  leading from, 37–38
  living your, 55–56, 61–63
  moving from *why* to, 53–55
  power of, 55
  statements of, 55–61
  why vs., 4
Because statements, 55–61
  Merritt's embodiment of, 58–61
  for team's sense of purpose, 38
  writing your, 56–58
Being who you are, 61–63
Belief in oneself, 60–61
Belonging *because* statement, 58, 59
Benefits, 58
Bezos, Jeff, 83
Blame, 85, 114–115
Brown, Les, 2
  on greatness within, 91
  learning from, 11–13
  vision of, 99
Business ownership, 8–10

C

Cancel culture, 112
Care, 16
  as crux in leadership, 10–11
  delegating with, 68–69
Careers, jobs vs., 15
Celebrating small wins, 116–117
Character, 6, 136
Checklists, 44–45
Collaboration, by Nexus Leaders, 163–169
Communication, 81–89
  assured vs. uncertain, 81–83
  by bad leaders, 85–87
  concrete vs. abstract, 83–84
  for confidence, 24–25
  during crises, 135
  difficult conversations, 118–120
  easily understandable, 83
  in leader voice, 88
  listening, 103–104
  low and slow speaking, 84–85
  rehearsing, 88–89
  taking action to improve, 89
  visioneering as, 95–97, 103–104
  with your team, 36
Community, being in, 59
Concrete communication, 83–84
Confidence in your abilities, 24–25
  hiding, 84
  self-deception about, 43–44
Conflict, growth from, 174–175
Consensus, building, 165–167

Continuous learning, 71–72, 122–123, 178
COVID-19 pandemic, 133–135
Credit, stealing, 113–114
Crisis leadership, 133–138
  and crises as moments of truth, 137–138
  mindfulness in, 136–137
Curiosity, 77

D

Delegation:
  with care, 68–69
  over-delegating, 48–49
  under-delegating, 49
Dictatorship:
  building consensus vs., 165–167
  strong leadership vs., 45–46
Difficult conversations, avoiding, 118–120
Distractions, leading without, 38–39
"Don't miss," 7

E

Easily understandable communication, 83
edX.org, 72
Effective leaders, 16
Ego, 21, 130, 173
Elevating your team, 173
Emotion, revealing, 82–83
Emotional intelligence, 34–35
Empathy:
  balancing structure and, 161
  communicating with, 96–97
  lack of, 50–52
  toward problem employees, 104–105
Empowerment:
  meaning of, 50
  over-delegation misperceived as, 48–50
  of your team, 77
The E-Myth (Gerber), 48
The E-Myth Revisited (Gerber), 66
Energy, of Ignitor Leaders, 151–156
Evolving, 177–178
"Execution time," 175
Experience, 12, 13, 75–76
Expertise:
  acknowledging lack of, 76
  embracing your, 67–68
  innovating through your, 73–74
  teaching others from your, 70–71
  of your team, trusting, 77

F

Feedback:
  in mastering leadership, 173–174
  requesting, 74–75
  resisting, 115–116
  seeking, 127
Forge Leaders:
  strengths and challenges of, 142

Forge Leaders (*Continued*)
  structure and precision of, 157–162
  weakness for, 177
Founding of America, 92
Four Leadership Archetypes, 139–143

G
Gandhi, Mahatma, 105
Gerber, Michael, 48, 66
Glover, Madison, 23–24, 37–38, 176–177
Goals:
  SMART, 153
  vague, 96–97
Good leaders:
  essential skills for, 65. *See also* Identifying core leadership strengths
  great leaders vs., 19–27
  great leaders who are not, 41–52
  seven *becauses* of, 53–63
  speaking and writing like, 81–89
Good leadership, 31–40
  balancing hard and soft power in, 34–35
  from *because*, 37–38
  essence of, 14
  and leadership vs. influence, 32–33
  try-hards vs., 33–34
  when young, 36–37
  without distractions, 38–39

Gratitude, 126–127
Great leaders:
  good leaders vs., 19–27
  inauthenticity of, 65
  limitations of, 31–40
  who aren't good leaders, *see* Bad leaders
Greatness, perception of, 26
Great people, 13
Growth:
  from conflict, 174–175
  leadership as journey of, 10–12
  mindset of, 24–25

H
Hard power, 32–34
Horizon Health Services, 24–25
Humble power, 33–35

I
Identifying core leadership strengths, 65–79
  balancing hands-on with oversight, 72–73
  continuous learning, 71–72
  delegating with care, 68–69
  embracing your expertise, 67–68
  innovating through your expertise, 73–74
  integrating non-leader skills into leadership roles, 66
  self-reflecting and requesting feedback, 74–75
  sharing like a mentor, 70–71
  time management, 69
  troubleshooting tips for, 75–78

Ignitor Leaders:
  energy and momentum of, 151–156
  strengths and challenges of, 141–142
  weakness for, 177
Impact, 6, 21
Influence, leadership vs., 32–33
Innovation, through your expertise, 73–74
Inspiration:
  motivation vs., 35
  self-promotion disguised as, 46–48
Isolating yourself, 117–118

J
Jobs, careers vs., 15
Jobs, Steve, 83
Judging in public, 112–113

K
King, Martin Luther, Jr., 92–93
Knowledge base. *See also* Expertise
  building, 76
  teaching others from your, 70–71

L
Leaders:
  bad, *see* Bad leaders
  great vs. good, 19–27. *See also* Good leaders; Great leaders
  with humble power, 34–35
  young, 35–37
Leadership, 10–12
  archetypes of, *see* Archetypes of leadership
  from *because,* 37–38
  bowing out of, *see* Leaving leadership positions
  core strengths for, *see* Identifying core leadership strengths
  growing into, 66
  influence vs., 32–33
  integrating non-leader skills into, 66
  under intense pressure, *see* Crisis leadership
  as journey of growth and self-discovery, 181
  mastering, 171–179
  trustworthy, *see* Trustworthy leadership rules
  without distractions, 38–39
Leadership DNA, 139–143
Leader voice, 88
Learning:
  continuous, 71–72, 122–123, 178
  quickly, 76
Leaving leadership positions, 125–132
  avoiding resentment when, 129–130
  gratitude in, 126–127
  mitigating regret when, 130–132
  passing the torch, 128–129

Legacy planning, 128–129
Leveraging leadership
 strengths, 76
Listening, 103–104
Love *because* statement, 57, 59
Lying, 110–111

M

Maslow, Abraham, 56
Maslow's hierarchy of needs, 56
Mastering leadership, 171–179
 elevating your team in, 173
 evolving in, 177–178
 feedback in, 173–174
 growth from conflict
  in, 174–175
 resilience mindset in, 175–176
 serving in, 176–177
 staying true to your
  core in, 177
 stewardship in, 172
 taking ownership in, 178–179
 vision followed by
  action in, 175
Maxwell, John, 12
Mental health training, 16
Mental resilience, 6, 39
Mentor(s):
 sharing like a, 70–71
 from within your team, 78
Merritt, Carlton, 58–61
MICK factor, 6
Mick Unplugged
 Community, 28–29
Micromanagement, 44–45, 73
Mindfulness, in a crisis, 136–137

Mindset:
 of growth, 24–25
 of resilience, 175–176
Mission statements, 37, 55
Moments of truth, crises as,
  137–138
Momentum:
 and feedback, 173–174
 of Ignitor Leaders, 151–156
Motivation(s):
 inspiration vs., 35
 levels of priority for, 56–57
 reflecting on your, 55
 for your *why*, 54
Motivational leadership
  videos, 31–33
Musk, Elon, 83, 93

N

Needs, hierarchy of, 56
Negativity:
 harnessing, 21
 redirecting, 105–106
Networking, 9, 78–79
Nexus Leaders:
 strengths and challenges
  of, 142–143
 trust and collaboration
  of, 163–169
 weakness for, 177

O

Omission, lying by, 111
Opinions of others, 26–27
Outsider perspective, 77–78
Over-delegation, 48–49

Overpromising and underdelivering, 42, 120–122
Oversight:
  balancing autonomy with, 77
  balancing hands-on with, 72–73
Ownership, 36, 178–179

P
Paradiso, Chris, 23, 36–37, 173
Paradiso Insurance, 23
Passing the torch, 128–129. *See also* Leaving leadership positions
Perception of greatness, 26
Permission, asking for, 82
Persuasion, 41–42
Physiological *because* statement, 57, 58
Pinnacle Marketing Solutions, 23–24
Positivity, about your vision, 97–98
Power:
  of *because*, 55
  to elevate others, 178–179
  hard vs. soft, 32–34
  humble, 33–35
Praising good work, 59
Precision, of Forge Leaders, 157–162
Premier Strategy Box, 11
Pride, when stepping aside, 129–130
Problem employees, 101–108
  empathy toward, 104–105
  example of, 106–108
  listening to, 103–104
  punishing, 102–105
  redirecting negativity of, 105–106
Problems solved, with vision, 93–94
Providing a haven, 58–59
Public judgment, 112–113
Punishing employees, 102–105
Purpose, articulating your, 55

R
Reasoning, surface-level, 54–55
Redirecting negativity, 105–106
Regret, when leaving leadership positions, 130–132
Rehearsing communications, 88–89
Resentment, when leaving leadership positions, 129–130
Resilience:
  mental, 6, 39
  mindset of, 175–176
Results, creating, 59–60
Reverse mentorship, 78
Role models, 19–20, 31

S
Safety *because* statement, 57, 58–59
Security *because* statement, 57, 58–59

Seeing the best in people, *see* Problem employees
Self-actualization *because* statement, 58, 60–61
Self-deception, 42–44
Self-discovery, leadership as journey of, 10–12
Self-esteem *because* statement, 58, 59–60
Self-promotion, 46–48
Self-reflection, 52, 74–75
Self-validation, 21
Self-worth, 21
Serving, 21, 176–177
Sharing, like a mentor, 70–71
Shiny-object syndrome, 36, 94–95
Simple English Wikipedia, 76
SMART goals, 153
Soft power, 32–34
Speaking, *see* Communication
Staying true to your core, 177
Stealing the credit, 113–114
Stewardship, 172
Strategy:
   of Apex Leaders, 145–150
   for Ignitor Leaders, 153
Strengths:
   identifying your, *see* Identifying core leadership strengths
   leveraging your, 76
   unique combinations of, *see* Archetypes of leadership
Strong leadership, dictatorship vs., 45–46
Structure, of Forge Leaders, 157–162
Summit Hospitality Group, 24
SWOT analysis, 130–131, 137

T

Teaching others, 70–71
Team:
   communicating with, 36
   elevating your, 173
   empowering your, 77
   seeking mentorship within, 78
   value of vision for, 95
Technical proficiency, 66–68. *See also* Expertise
Tesla Motors, 93
Time management, 69, 95
Toughness, perceiving lack of empathy as, 50–51
Trust:
   of Nexus Leaders, 163–169
   in team's expertise, 77
Trust and verify, 77
Trustworthy leadership rules, 109–123
   don't lie, even by omission, 110–111
   never avoid difficult conversations, 118–120
   never blame, 114–115
   never isolate yourself, 117–118
   never judge in public, 112–113
   never neglect continuous learning, 122–123
   never overlook small wins, 116–117

never overpromise and
    underdeliver, 120–122
never resist feedback, 115–116
never steal the credit, 113–114
Try-hards, 33–34

U

Uncertainty:
    in communicating, 81–83
    with lack of vision, 95
Under-delegating, 49

V

Vermost, Darren, 22, 34–35,
    61–62
Vermost Insurance Agency, 22
Visibility to employees, 117–118
Vision, 91–99
    of Apex Leaders, 145–150
    being positive about
        your, 97–98
    of Brown, 99
    direction created by, 89
    followed by action,
        91–92, 98, 175
    problem solved by, 93–95
    reality and, 175
    visioneering of, 95–97
Visioneering, 95–97, 103–104

Vision statements, 37, 55, 98
"Vision time," 175
Vitali, Mark, 9, 10
Voice:
    leader, 88
    low and slow, 84–85

W

Walkabouts, 117–118
Why:
    because vs., 4
    moving to *because* from, 53–54
    problems when starting
        with, 54–55
    team's understanding of
        your, 37–38
    without a *because,* 43
Williams, Rebecca, 24–25,
    38–39, 133–135, 175–176
Will to keep going, 6
Wins:
    acknowledging, 127
    celebrating, 116–117
Wisdom, 12–13
Woods, Tiger, 82
Worth as a leader, 21
Wright, Edward "Eddie,"
    14–16, 24
Writing, *see* Communication